The Tealover's Companion

Throughout my writing career, I have always been amazed at people's kindness and willingness to help. For this particular book, my sincere thanks go to first and foremost Bruce Richardson who, with his wife Shelley, has become a close friend over the past few years and whose information, advice, support and brilliant photography help to make this book what it is.

Thanks also to ~
Dan Robertson, owner of The Tea House in Naperville, Illinois, who supplied the rare China and Taiwan teas photographed by Bruce and his son Ben. Dan also gave me vital information about tea production in China and Taiwan.

All the team at St James's Teas and Wilson Smithett, who have supported this project from the start and supplied teas for photography.

Various friends in the world of tea who have supplied photographs – Nigel Melican of Teacraft, Alan Hobbs of Lawrie Plantation Group, Ashok Kumar of Marco Polo Products, Dilmah Teas and Karl Attard. And finally, the team at National Trust Publications, especially Fiona Screen, Matt Bourne and Helen Cross, who worked so hard to create what I feel is a book that we can all be proud of.

Jane Pettigrew, 2005

The Tealover's Companion

A Guide to Teas throughout the World

Jane Pettigrew & Bruce Richardson

 THE NATIONAL TRUST

First published in Great Britain in 2005 by
National Trust Enterprises Ltd
36 Queen Anne's Gate
London
SW1H 9AS

ISBN 0 7078 0390 X

Cataloguing in Publication Data is available from the British Library.

Editor: Fiona Screen
Book design & typesetting: Matt Bourne
Set in Perpetua

Origination by Digital Imaging Ltd, Glasgow
Printed and bound in Hong Kong by Printing Express

The author and publishers would like to thank the following institutions and individuals for their kind permission to reproduce illustrations:

Guildhall Library, Corporation of London page 57; Karl Attard pages 52, 56; Richard l'Anson/Lonely Planet Images page 142, Martin Moos/Lonely Planet Images page 154; Mary Evans Picture Library pages 1, 6, 10, 12, 17, 20, 23, 55, 60, 126, 165, 166; National Trust Photographic Library page 14; Jane Pettigrew pages 7, 25, 46, 67, 70, 75; Bruce Richardson pages 27, 29, 30−1, 34, 36, 39−42, 48−51, 53, 58, 61, 62, 64, 68, 71, 73, 111, 146, 167, 173; © Teacraft Ltd pages 106, 134, 138

All tea shots in Directory pages by Bruce Richardson

Maps © Oxford Designers and Illustrators

Frontispiece ~ A late 19th-century hand-coloured photograph of Japanese ladies taking tea

Contents

Tea's Origins in China

Anyone who has any interest at all in tea, no matter how new or how small, cannot fail to recognize the fascinating links between modern tea-drinking and Ancient China. The story weaves its way so far back through Chinese history (2737BC is the date always mentioned as the starting point) that it is impossible to know the true facts, and so stories and legends have grown up to explain the discovery, early cultivation and consumption of this wonderful life-enhancing beverage. Tea's journey through the ages and across every continent has inevitably meant the gradual development of new production methods, new rituals and new, inventive pieces of equipage, but we cannot deny its colourful and intriguing origins.

A Chinese tea plantation c.1840

The accepted myths and legends tell us that it was Shen Nung, emperor, scholar and herbalist, who first recognized tea's healthful properties and refreshingly delicious taste when a few stray leaves drifted down from an overhanging tree one day and fell by chance into the cauldron of water that he was boiling. Other stories of tea's discovery have been told over the centuries, but all praise tea's ability to alleviate drowsiness and assist concentration, to restore energy, combat depression and revive the spirit. Recognized from the earliest days as a tonic herb, tea was taken internally by the Chinese as a digestive aid and applied topically in ointments to alleviate skin troubles and rheumatism.

During the rule of the Han Dynasty (AD206–220), tea became more and more popular and today antique lacquer tea trays and tables, decorated lacquer cups and early porcelain tea bowls from the period bear witness to the drink's widespread use. It is thought that until this time wild tea trees had been felled so that the leaves might be stripped off for brewing and, as demand for the raw material grew, plantations were established for commercial cultivation. This, and improved methods of manufacture, helped to guarantee a regular, good-quality crop and allow the growth of a thriving trade throughout China which earned fortunes for the traders.

By the end of the 3rd century AD, tea had become China's national drink and in AD332 the first record of tea manufacture was written by Zhang Yi, giving details of how plants were laid out, pruned and plucked, and how the leaves were processed. During the 4th and 5th centuries, many new plantations were established along the Yangtze River Valley, and tea was now consumed not simply as a tonic brew but as a pleasurable drink. During the Tang Dynasty (AD618–906), a strict code of tea etiquette evolved and a new professional class of Tea Masters acquired an important role in society as employees of the emperor and wealthy mandarins. During the reign of the Song Dynasty (AD960–1279), the Chinese Tea-house became the focus of Chinese social life and a venue for merchants and dealers, friends and families, to gather and talk business, chat, relax, play cards or chess, and enjoy the professional storytellers, poets, jugglers and actors who entertained there.

During the 8th century AD, Lu Yu, China's first real tea specialist and known today as 'the patron saint of tea', wrote his *Cha Chang* (Classic of Tea). Having learnt how to brew tea correctly from his adoptive father, a

Lu Yu, one of the earliest writers on tea

Buddhist monk, Lu Yu worked for twenty years to produce a work that became essential reading for tea farmers, tea merchants and the consuming Chinese public. In the *Cha Chang* he described the plant and its cultivation, the way in which different teas are manufactured, instructed readers as to what sort of water to use for brewing, and examined the culture and rituals of tea-drinking, and the health benefits that make it a perfect beverage.

The Chinese were by now trading their tea to Arab lands to the East, Persia to the West, to Tibet, to the Turks, to tribes and groups living in the Himalayas and along the 'Silk Road' trading route that linked India to Macedonia. Trade with Europe started in the late 16th century but the long sea voyages often resulted in deterioration of the tea and forced the Chinese tea producers to find ways of improving manufacture, packaging and transportation. Until this point in tea's history, all Chinese teas were green and under the Ming Dynasty (AD1368–1644), instead of being formed into dried compressed cakes as in previous times, the delicate dried leaf was sold loose and consequently was easily spoiled before it reached the customer. So the profit-conscious Chinese producers devised a method of manufacturing black teas. This meant that the leaf lasted longer and travelled better. To make black tea they allowed the leaves to oxidize naturally before drying them to a dark coppery colour. The Chinese people continued to drink green tea but the new black variety found burgeoning markets as European trading companies imported increasing supplies to their home ports.

How the Chinese Drank their Tea

Until the 3rd century AD, under the Han Dynasty (AD206–220) the Chinese drank tea as a medicinal tonic brew made from the freshly gathered leaves of the wild tea tree. For the next 700 or so years, the plucked leaves were steamed and then compressed into tightly packed cakes of different forms which could be easily stored or transported with minimum damage. To brew tea from these cakes, the brick or cake was roasted and then chopped or crushed, and steeped or boiled in hot water. The infusion was then often flavoured with sweet onions, salt, ginger, orange peel, cloves or mint.

During the days of the Song Dynasty (AD960–1279), the compressed cakes developed a characteristic triangular shape and were crushed and steeped in the same way, but spicy flavouring was now abandoned in favour of gentler additions such as jasmine, lotus and chrysanthemum flowers. It was during this period that powdered tea also became popular.

The gathering of the leaf and the processing of the tea demanded great patience and skill. The young shoots of exclusive bushes were carefully plucked and then stored inside airtight jars for several months. The dried leaves were then ground to a fine powder which was whisked into hot water to give a frothy liquid. Depending on the buds that had been gathered, the colour of the whisked tea varied from exquisite white to a rich jade green. Up to seven fresh additions of water were poured onto the residue of the ground tea to give a different colour and flavour at each whisking.

Under the Ming Dynasty (AD 1368–1644), although some tea was still compressed into cakes and bricks, the fashion for loose tea gradually developed. The leaves were plucked, dried and shaped and then stored loose in sealed earthenware or lacquer chests. To brew the tea, the whole leaves were steeped in boiling water inside earthenware or porcelain teapots – the method of preparation copied by European drinkers when early supplies of the loose tea began to arrive in Amsterdam, Lisbon and London.

Beyond China's Borders

It is hard to know when the Mongolians and Tibetans learned to drink tea from the Chinese but it was probably in the 2nd or 3rd century AD. Compressed cakes of dried tea from China were transported by camel and the brew became the national drink of both races. Turkish traders are also recorded as having bartered for tea on the Mongolian border in the late 6th century and today tea is far more important than coffee in Turkey, despite popular belief. Trade with the Arab world started in the 5th and 6th centuries AD but there is no proof that tea was amongst the goods sold until the reign of Kublai Khan in the 13th century.

In the 8th century AD, the Japanese discovered the benefits of tea-drinking from the Chinese as a result of contact between Buddhist priests from the two countries. In AD 729, the Japanese emperor, Shomu, is said to have served tea to one hundred Buddhist monks at his palace in Nara. In the early 9th century, the Buddhist monk Dengyo Daishi carried some tea seeds home with him from China (where he had been studying) and planted them in the garden of his monastery. The plants were carefully tended for five years and then the first harvest of leaves and buds was gathered and used to brew tea for the Emperor Saga. The emperor was apparently so delighted with the beverage that he gave instructions for five plantations to be established for the commercial cultivation of the bushes. Tea became the favourite drink of Japanese Buddhist monks who found that it helped them to stay awake during long periods of prayer and meditation but, due to a cooling in Chinese–Japanese relations from the 9th to the 11th centuries, tea fell from favour at court and was no longer consumed. In 1191, another Japanese monk, Yeisai-zenji, returned from China after studying Zen Buddhism there and brought with him not just more

Preparing for the elaborate Japanese Tea Ceremony

tea seeds but the new method of whisking powdered tea into hot water and the serving and drinking rituals developed by the Chinese Rinzai Zen Buddhist sect. Although that particular method of preparing powdered tea died away in China as steeped tea became fashionable, the Japanese adapted and developed it into a formalized and complicated ceremony. By the 15th century, the Japanese Tea Ceremony, *Cha-no-yu* (see page 74), was firmly established as an ideal tea-drinking event governed by precise rules. Three schools of tea were set up by the Zen Buddhist priests: Ikkyu, Shuko and Rikkyu.

Tea Reaches Europe

We know that China was trading with Greece in the 2nd century BC, and that the Han Dynasty was investigating the possibility of trading with the Roman Empire in the 1st century AD, but there is no mention of tea in records of the time. During the 6th and 7th centuries, the Arabs had a monopoly over trade between China and the West and there is still no record of tea having changed hands. Marco Polo arrived in China in 1271 but still no tea is mentioned.

Then, in 1559, Giambattista Ramusio, an Italian civil servant, wrote that a Persian traveller by the name of Hajji Mahommed had told him of Chai Catai, a herb used by the people of Szechwan Province in China to make a medicine for stomach ache and gout. From that point on, we find several references that indicate a growing awareness of tea (though still no record that any actually arrived in a European port). The Portuguese set up a trading base on the Canton river in 1557 but shipped no tea. The Dutch, however, with their first trading base established at Bantam on the island of Java, sent their first cargo of China tea to Amsterdam in 1606. The Dutch people began to show an interest in this new herb in the 1630s, as indicated in a letter from the directors of the Dutch East India Company in 1637 to their Governor-general in Batavia: 'As tea begins to come into use with some of the people, we expect some jars of Chinese, as well as Japanese tea with each ship.'

In Holland, the newly imported tea was sold in apothecaries' shops and later in early grocery shops known as 'colonial warehouses'. The Dutch writer Jan Nieuhoff helped raise awareness of the herb at home and elsewhere after he met the Manchu rulers in Peking and experienced Chinese tea-drinking at first hand:

> There is a great difference in the manner of preparing and using this liquor between the Chinese and those of Japan; for the Japanese beat the leaves into a powder and mingle it with boiling water in a cup which they afterwards drink off; but the Chinese put the leaves whole into a pot of boiling water, which having lain in steep for some time they sip it hot, without swallowing down any of the leaves, but only the Quintessence thereof extracted.

He also explained how the Manchus themselves prepared their tea:

> They infuse half a handful of the herb Thea or Cha in fair water which
> they afterwards boil till a third part be consumed, to which they add
> warm milk about a fourth part, with a little salt, and then drink it as
> hot as they can well endure.

By the mid-1600s interest among the wealthy upper classes of Europe
– for tea was a costly indulgence – was beginning to grow and so the
Dutch decided to re-export the tea they had shipped from China into
Portugal, Germany and France. In France, in 1648, tea was referred to by
a Parisian doctor as 'the impertinent novelty of the age'; the playwright
Racine drank copious quantities; Cardinal Mazarin drank it as a cure for
gout; and in 1684, in a letter to her daughter, Madame de Sévigné recommended that tea should be drunk with both milk and sugar. However,
despite its favoured position in France as the most fashionable drink of the
1680s, tea quickly gave way to coffee, never to regain its early popularity.
In Germany, tea was at first drunk as a medicinal brew but, as in France,
did not capture the long-term attention of the German people except in
what is now called East-Freisia, in the northern part of the country, where
tea has for more than 300 years been the chosen beverage. In Portugal, as
in Holland, tea became a luxury beverage for members of the court and
the wealthy upper classes, and it was here that Catherine of Braganza (see
page 14), who was later to marry the English King Charles II, learned to
love it. When she travelled to England in 1662 for her wedding she
brought with her, as part of her dowry, ownership of the islands of
Bombay and a casket of tea!

The first tea reached Russia in the early 17th century when the
Mongolian ruler, Altyun-Khan, sent a gift of tea to Tsar Michael
Fedorovich. Meanwhile, the signing of the Treaty of Nerchinska in 1689
marked the beginning of regular trade between the two countries. At first
the drink was consumed only by the Russian élite but gradually other
social groups discovered it and developed their own ways of brewing and
serving the infusion. Until the late 18th century, supplies were transported to the Russian market by camels pulling caravans along the 'Great
Tea Road' which ran from Kashgar behind China's Great Wall, through the

Gobi Desert to Urga in Mongolia. At Usk Kayakhta, the teas were inspected and packed into paper and foil packages which were then stowed inside bamboo boxes, and loaded onto sledges and carts. From here, the laborious journey took between 16 and 18 months. It is said that 'Russian Caravan' tea acquired its slightly smoky flavour from the smouldering fires that kept the travellers warm at night during essential periods of rest and sleep. As demand for tea in Russia grew, quantities rose to more than 6,000 camel-loads a year. This made the transportation so expensive that traders were forced out of business, leaving a vacuum that was quickly filled by English and German merchants. In 1903, the opening of the Trans-Siberian railway made it possible to transport goods from China much more rapidly than by ship to London, Amsterdam or Lisbon, and oriental products now arrived in Moscow, Paris and Berlin in just over a week.

Transporting tea across the Siberian highlands by camel

Tea for the British

An English collector of travellers' tales by the name of Samuel Purchas mentioned in 1625 in *Purchas His Pilgrimes* that the Chinese 'use much the powder of a certaine herbe called chia of which they put as much as a walnut shell may containe, into a dish of Porcelane, and drink it with hot water…'. In 1637, the Cornish traveller Peter Mundy wrote that the people of Fukien in China's Fujian Province 'gave us a certain Drinke called Chaa which is only water with a kind of herb boyled in it'.

So when Thomas Garraway started offering tea for sale at his general store in Exchange Alley in the City of London in 1657, it was not a totally unknown drink, but still Garraway recognized the need to advertise and, in 1660, wrote his famous broadsheet entitled *An Exact Description of the Growth, Quality and Vertues of the Leaf Tea*. In it he explained where tea came from, how it was produced and why it was good for you. Fourteen clauses claimed that tea would cure headaches, kidney problems, skin complaints, loss of memory, breathing difficulties, infections, drowsiness, insomnia, runny noses, watery eyes, aches and pains, fevers and colds, dropsy and scurvy. But tea, a rare oriental luxury, was expensive and made more so by a heavy tax imposed by the government, so Garraway's customers were at first few and far between and came occasionally from their aristocratic houses and palaces to buy half a pound or less at a time. With prices ranging from 16 to 60 shillings (equivalent to $1.44 to $5.40) a pound and average wages for servants such as butlers and footmen at £2 to £6 per year, it was only the Royal Family, wealthy members of the upper classes and highly paid civil servants who could afford such a commodity.

Catherine of Braganza, an early champion of tea in Europe

Catherine of Braganza inadvertently helped tea's cause when she arrived to marry King Charles II in 1662. Coming as she did from Portugal, one of the first countries to import tea into Europe, Catherine had grown up drinking tea and was an avid fan. The precious tea inside the casket that she brought with her to England was brewed by her for her friends at court and so the new herb became a distinctly fashionable treat. Ladies drank their tea at home in their closets while their menfolk went off to the coffee houses to drink tea, coffee or chocolate (and various alcoholic beverages) with their professional colleagues and friends. Coffee houses had opened in the 1650s, first in Oxford and Cambridge and then in London, and served hot beverages and a range of beers, ales, ciders, wines, sherries, ports, possets and sherbets.

The first tea brought into London in the 1650s was not imported by an English company but by the Dutch East India Company, and it was not until 1669 that the English East India Company ordered its first cargo of 143 pounds. With the price of tea remaining high, demand was small, and when the Company shipped in large quantities, the result was a glut of tea on the London market. The high cost of tea continued into the 18th century, with the tax at 14 per cent on all tea imported by the East India Company plus an additional 5 shillings or so in the pound payable by the purchaser.

Because of its high cost, tea had, from its earliest arrival in England, developed close associations with stately homes, palaces, expensive furnishings, fine linens and tablewares, and stylish living. Upper-class families acquired fine porcelains, silverwares and expensive imported tea tables in order to display their good taste, status and wealth. Shelves in the closets of large country houses held porcelain tea jars imported from China, small earthenware and porcelain teapots and the little bowls and saucers used for drinking the brew.

At Ham House near Richmond in Surrey, the Duchess of Lauderdale ensured that she owned all the necessary tea equipage for those frequent visits from her friend Queen Catherine. A fine wooden tea table from Java had extra length added to its legs in order to make it the perfect height for tea. The closet contained a silver 'Indian furnace' for boiling the water and a lacquered box that held the tea and porcelain teapots and bowls. Despite the risk of burnt fingers, the Duchess sometimes served tea in unusual silver tea bowls.

At Saltram House in Devon, Chinese wallpaper showing the various stages of tea manufacture decorated the walls of the Chinese Chippendale Bedroom, while in other parts of this elegant Georgian house, cabinets and shelves held early examples of European and English pottery, as well as stoneware teapots and tea bowls, Chinese porcelain tea jars decorated with roses, and lidded tea bowls covered with butterflies and delicate oriental flowers.

As the wealthier classes bought more and more green and black leaf, and the poorer classes began to get a taste for the brew, black market traders developed a thriving system of smuggling and illicit distribution to meet the demand. Tea was much cheaper in Holland and France where taxation was lower, and entire communities in England (including priests, politicians and other upstanding members of the community) were involved in concealing, storing, buying and selling the illegal imports from those European countries. To benefit from high prices, unscrupulous merchants mixed the real leaf with the treated leaves of other plants and bushes, or purchased used leaves and dyed them back to the original colour using copperas (ferrous sulphate) and sheep's dung, molasses and clay, before drying and selling them on. The government attempted to stamp out such unacceptable practices by introducing fines of £100 for smugglers and traders of 'smouch'. Punishment became more severe in 1730 when the fine was increased to £10 per pound of tea. It was generally easier to produce polluted or 'fake' green tea, and a trend towards the safer black variety became evident – the start, perhaps, of Britain's preference for black leaf.

By the middle of the 18th century, tea had become the preferred drink of all classes in Britain. Ale and beer at breakfast had generally been replaced by tea; visitors to upper-class palaces, castles and manor houses were offered the brew; tea was served after the main meal of the day as a 'digestif' to help settle the stomach after copious amounts of rich food; tea provided refreshment in the workplace and paid part of the servants' wages; a cup was included with the entrance fee in the pleasure gardens of London; and it was available in inns and taverns for travellers. And while tea gradually became the drink of the British people, consumed in homes and workplaces across the land, the upper classes continued to brew and serve the beverage as an elegant refreshment in their stately homes. In the gardens of such homes, temples and follies that had once served as banqueting houses (where sweetmeats and desserts were served after dinner) now became the favourite venues for tea. Once the main meal was over, the assembled party would stroll through the gardens to the orangery, or tea-room, miniature castle, rustic cottage or 'temple', where tea was served. At Cliveden in Buckinghamshire, Lord Orkney and his guests took tea in the Octagon temple, a two-storey building set on the edge of an escarpment overlooking the River Thames. Designed by the Venetian architect Giacomo Leoni, this charming building contained a small room (known as 'the grotto') on the lower level where tea equipage was stored, and an upper room, The Prospect Room, where guests drank tea and enjoyed the view. At Saltram House in Devon, 'The Castle' provided the perfect location for visitors to relax and take tea while admiring the beautifully landscaped gardens.

Until the early 19th century all the tea drunk in Britain was imported from China, carried exclusively on the ships of the English East India Company. But trade with China was becoming more and more expensive and problems were developing because of the trading of opium – an illegal but widely used drug in China. The East India Company was selling into China opium that had been grown on British territory in India, and in 1839 the exasperated Chinese emperor ordered 20,000 chests to be deposited on the beach so that it would be washed away by the tide.

In 1840, the British declared war on the Chinese and the Chinese retaliated by imposing an embargo on tea exports to Britain. Fortunately, by then the tea plant had been found growing in north-eastern India, the first plantations had been established in Assam and the first British-grown Assam tea had reached the London tea auctions in 1839. During the 1850s, the gardens of Darjeeling were planted, and cultivation spread up into Terai and Dooars in the 1860s. Trials were carried out in southern India in the 1830s but commercial production did not really get going there until the 1890s.

In Ceylon, now Sri Lanka, the first plantations were laid out in the late 1860s and by 1900 roughly 155,000 hectares (380,000 acres) of land were given over to tea. With more and more British-grown tea and less and less being imported from China, prices began to drop and tea truly became the everyday drink of the British people.

Before the production of tea in India and Ceylon made tea more readily available and increased British consumption, the speedy clipper ships of the 1840s, '50s and early '60s had played their part in the tea story by dramatically reducing the journey time from the Chinese ports. The name was first used in the mid-1840s to describe American vessels and probably derives from the equestrian term 'to go at a good clip'. Initially 'clipper' referred to almost any vessel that sped across water at an unusually fast pace, but gradually people started talking of coffee clippers, Californian clippers, tea clippers and China clippers. These sleek, elegant ships were built for speed and, while traditional cargo ships sailed at less than 5 knots, clippers achieved up to 18 knots. In 1845, the American clipper the *Baltimore* completed the round trip from New York to China in just eight months. The British soon recognized the need to build their own clippers to compete and the *Stornaway* was launched from Aberdeen in 1850. The

The Tea Clipper 'Ariel', from a Wills's cigarette card of 1866

race for time and the promised high prices for the first teas home meant that competition between the clippers built to an annual frenzy. Brokers would camp out in the London docks ready to taste and bid for the best of the new arrivals. In 1866, in the most

WILLS'S CIGARETTES.

famous race of all, 40 vessels took part. Three ships, the *Taeping*, the *Ariel* and the *Serica,* sailed almost dead level right across the Indian Ocean and, 99 days after setting sail from the Canton river, the *Taeping* and the *Ariel* docked within 20 minutes of each other, with the *Serica* coming in just a few hours later. In 1871 the last of the clipper races thrilled the British public, by which time the Suez Canal had opened and steamships were carrying goods more quickly by that route.

Although by the beginning of the 19th century people across Britain were consuming growing quantities of tea, there was still no formalized 'afternoon tea' as we now know it. The credit for 'inventing' this now famous institution is often given to Anna Maria, 7th Duchess of Bedford, in the 1840s, but in fact she did not create a new meal, but merely renamed a social occasion that was already evolving because of changing mealtimes. In the 17th century, dinner was served at midday and lasted for four or five hours. This was followed by tea-drinking, accompanied by thinly sliced bread and butter, in the withdrawing room. As the years passed, the dinner hour grew later and later until, in the 1820s and '30s, it was served at 7.30, 8 or even 8.30pm. With breakfast at 9 or 9.30am, and only a very light meal at midday in the form of the newly invented luncheon (also called 'nuncheon' or 'noonshine'), there was a long gap until dinner with no refreshment or sustenance. And so the Duchess and others like her called for their tea equipage in order to brew a private cup of tea in the boudoir or drawing room. Once Anna Maria had made the idea fashionable by inviting her aristocratic friends to join her for a cup of 'afternoon tea', such social gatherings became an essential part of British life amongst upper-, middle- and working-class ladies. By the late 1860s, cookery books and manuals of household management were giving detailed instructions on how to organize a tea party, what foods to serve, the duties of the servants, where to place the furniture, what to wear, what entertainment to arrange, how to set out the tray, where to stand to receive guests, and at what time guests should arrive and depart.

At stately homes and country mansions throughout the land, tea parties became a regular occurrence and were often devised around a particular occasion – a birthday, a wedding, a fashionable sporting event, or perhaps a royal visit. At Waddesdon Manor in Buckinghamshire, the Rothschild family entertained the Prince and Princess of Wales to tea in the garden. A striped marquee was erected for the occasion and sat majestically on the lawn in front of the elegant towers of the house while the royal visitors relaxed in cane chairs and sipped their afternoon tea from fine bone china cups. In grand houses all over the country, China closets held several different tea sets in various designs with enough plates, cups and saucers to serve tea to at least twelve guests. At Tatton Park in Cheshire, the numerous tea sets included a 900-piece service in glass. An 1871 household inventory from Dyrham Park near Bath details a pink and white service, a blue and gold service, a white service, a tea service with a 'sprig pattern' and a service with a pink border, showing how important tea had become in the life of the country house.

In contrast to the elegance and refinement of 'afternoon tea', the Industrial Revolution had led to the development of a working-class evening meal called 'high tea', a robust and satisfying spread of hearty foods, accompanied by a pot of strong tea, served at 5.30 or 6pm and designed to welcome workers home from their long shifts in factories, mines, workshops and offices. Whereas the point of afternoon tea was to gossip and chat, show off the latest fashions and sip tea, the point of high tea was to replace all the calories that had been burned up during a 10- or 12-hour shift of hard manual work. And while afternoon tea was and still is served in the drawing room or garden, with guests seated in low armchairs and sofas, high tea is served in the kitchen or dining room, with the family seated in high-backed chairs around the table.

Taking tea had been a popular part of the entertainment provided in the pleasure gardens of 18th-century London, but with the expansion of the suburbs and the building of new roads and houses, the gardens gradually closed. By the time 'afternoon tea' had become a part of British social life, there was nowhere to go 'out to tea'. That all changed in the 1870s and '80s when tea-rooms started to appear, first in Glasgow and then in London and other provincial towns. Stuart Cranston and his sister Kate were pioneers in Scotland, while in London the Aerated Bread Company (ABC) served the first cups of tea in 1884 at the London Bridge branch of their bread and cake company. Other companies quickly set up their own successful tea-rooms in town while in rural Britain cottage gardens were converted into tea gardens where local farmers' wives and country ladies and their daughters would scurry to and fro with pots of tea, scones,

Miss Cranston's famous tea-rooms in Glasgow, designed by Rennie Mackintosh

biscuits and home-made cakes to satisfy the hunger and thirst of day-trippers, cyclists and walkers.

As tea became more and more popular, new tea trading companies were established all around Britain, allowing successful entrepreneurs to make small fortunes from their dealings in tea and other groceries. Julius Drewe founded the once famous Home and Colonial Stores in 1885 and made tea the most important of the shops' products, with high-quality Indian teas at the top of the list. Within four years, Drewe owned 43 branches across Britain and managed to amass a fortune that allowed him to build Castle Drogo in Devon (designed by Sir Edwin Lutyens) and retire at the age of 33 to live the life of a country gentleman.

When the Edwardian period brought a new fashion for travelling and stylish living, luxury hotels offered comfort and refinement like never before. All had a tea lounge or palm court where every day at 4 o'clock tea would be served to the accompanying strains of a string quartet or palm court trio. During this period, tea-time took an eccentric turn by incorporating dancing into the afternoon event. Afternoon tea at home had often included musical entertainment and sometimes 'dancing on the carpet' but when the tango arrived in 1910 from Argentina, it shocked and thrilled everyone with its risqué steps and erotic style. By 1913 there were tango clubs and classes throughout London and people were flocking to tango tea dances in hotels, theatres and restaurants.

Changes in social patterns, due mainly to two world wars and the introduction in the 1950s of American-style fast-food restaurants and coffee bars, meant that tea-rooms gradually disappeared from the high street. Although the British did not stop drinking tea at home, the earlier fashion for going out to tea, tea dances and tea parties had gradually declined and tea began to play a less prominent role in the nation's social life. With the introduction of American-style coffee bars, fast-food restaurants and teabags, most tea-rooms closed down and catering outlets seemed to forget how to serve good tea. Then, in the early 1980s, there began a gradual reawakening of interest in tea, with new tea shops opening, new books published, tea dances in London hotels attracting eager guests on Saturday and Sunday afternoons, and a realization that some of us were actually rather tired of self-service, fast-food outlets, plastic table-tops, greasy food and badly brewed tea. Since then, many new tea-rooms have opened around Britain and hotels have improved their afternoon tea service. Instead of teabags, caterers are realizing that they must choose quality loose-leaf tea, brew and serve the tea well, make tea foods more exciting and appetizing by introducing flavoured breads for the sandwiches, light, home-made scones, exquisite pastries and cakes, and sometimes little extra treats such as mini crème brulées or sorbets or, in summer, dishes of strawberries and cream. And for those who wish to brew good tea at home, new retailers have made quality loose-leaf teas more readily available in the high street, supermarkets have increased their range of teas, and the internet now brings us mail order teas at the click of the mouse. With increased coverage in the press and a growing interest in quality and choice, tea is once again attracting the attention it deserves.

Tea in North America

As migrant groups for Europe set sail for the new continent in the late 17th and 18th centuries, they carried with them their most vital and prized household objects, including their tea things. In 1650, Peter Stuyvesant brought the first tea to the Dutch in their newly established colony, New Amsterdam, and when the British took control of the city in

1674 and renamed it New York, they found that tea-drinking was already firmly established and as important there as in Europe. Good-quality drinking water was not readily available in the city and so special water pumps were installed. Coffee houses and tea gardens became popular gathering places, just as in England, with New York boasting its own 'Vauxhall Gardens', or 'Ranelagh'.

In the different regions of the new colonies, settlers drank tea according to their individual lifestyles. In elegant homes, tea was brewed in porcelain teapots and drunk from fine European cups and saucers, while country folk boiled their kettles on the open fire of the kitchen range and measured the loose leaf into humble pottery teapots. In 1670, residents of Boston became aware of tea but the trade there was not established until the 1690s. By the 1720s and '30s, it had become a fashionable and popular drink and both Boston and Philadelphia acquired reputations for fancy tea parties and perfect tea-time manners, with tea-drinking closely associated with good breeding and social status. Tea was still expensive and very much an upper-class luxury. As in England, wealthy households boasted fine porcelains imported from China, silverware fashioned by European and American silversmiths, fancy lace cloths and little silver teaspoons, pretty dishes for bread and butter and tea tables upon which to arrange the necessary tablewares.

The wealthy cities of New York, Boston and Philadelphia became centres for the trade, and tea and tea equipage now featured prominently on lists of items traded from Britain to the American colony. But because tea was so heavily taxed by Britain at the time, it was smuggled into other ports from Europe by independent merchants and the British government lost as much revenue here because of black market trading as it was losing at home. Total consumption in the colony was over a million pounds of tea each year, but only a quarter of this was actually traded from London. The rest was smuggled. In 1767, a temporary solution was found whereby London merchants could claim a refund of taxes if tea was re-exported to America. Prices fell and over half a million pounds of tea were 'officially' shipped into American ports. The following year, the amount rose further to 900,000 pounds.

The success was short-lived. After the high costs of the war against the French and the Native Americans that gave Britain control of the colony, the British government was eager to raise funds and proposed a tax on British goods imported into America. This resulted in a boycott of British goods and general unrest, and when a further direct tax of 3 pence in the pound was subsequently imposed on tea to raise money for the upkeep of British soldiers and civil servants stationed in the colony, the colonialists were inflamed. Since the British East India Company still held a monopoly on trade of tea into America, there was no way to avoid the tax, and tea exports from Britain to America fell dramatically to just 226,156 pounds in 1769 and 108,629 pounds in 1770, while smuggling once again increased.

In February 1773, the directors of the East India Company sought permission from the government to ship some of its by now surplus stock to America and, with amazing lack of foresight, the Tea Act was passed that allowed the Company to send four ships, carrying a total of more than 100,000 pounds of tea, across the Atlantic. The rest is history. In New York and Philadelphia, shipments of tea were forced to turn back. In Charleston, customs officials seized the cargo. In Boston, when the *Dartmouth* arrived carrying 114 chests of tea, she tied up at Griffin's Wharf, the tea was entered at customs and the ship then lay in Boston Harbour for three weeks while unrest amongst the locals grew. Eight days later the *Eleanor* sailed into port and the *Beaver* tied up on 15

The Boston Tea Party ~ Boston's citizens, dressed as Native Americans, boarded East India Company ships and threw tea chests into the sea.

December. Enough was enough! On the night of 16 December 1773, to cries of 'Boston harbor a teapot tonight' and 'The Mohawks are coming', the three ships were boarded by a band of men disguised as Native Americans and for the following three hours 340 chests of tea were split open with hatchets and the tea hurled overboard into Boston harbour. The British closed the port and sent troops in to occupy the city. And so it was that a major error of judgement over The Tea Act of 1773 led to the

American War of Independence and the ultimate loss to the British crown of the American colonies.

Following Boston, exhortations were issued to all Americans to 'Throw aside your Bohea and your Green Hyson tea, And all things with a new-fangled duty', and the ladies of Boston declared that they had bid:

> Farewell the Tea-board with your gaudy attire,
> Ye cups and ye saucers that I did admire;
> To my cream pots and tongs I now bid adieu
> The pleasure's all fled that I once found in you …

However, tea did not disappear from American homes altogether. Direct trade with China was established in 1784 and George Washington, first President of the United States of America and an avid tea-drinker, gave instructions during the War of Independence which ensured that all officers and men received a regular supply of tea. At home he continued to serve his favourite beverage to guests at his home at Mount Vernon.

In the early part of the 19th century, the introduction of faster American sailing ships by the newly established American tea merchants, together with the 'clippers' of the 1840s, made transportation of tea from China to the United States much faster and allowed the American traders to cut deeply into Britain's markets.

By the turn of the 20th century, America was confident and strong enough economically to hold the St Louis World's Fair in 1904. Traders and merchants from all over the world exhibited and it was here that Richard Blechynden, an English tea-planter, popularized iced tea. It was probably down to Blechynden that iced tea is as important to Americans today as hot tea has always been to the British. His original plan to offer samples of hot Indian tea to the visiting public was thwarted by exceptionally hot weather and so he served what he had brewed in glasses packed with plenty of ice. Iced tea and iced tea punches had actually been included in cookery books since the 1830s, after the invention of ice boxes, but Blechynden brought them to the notice of the general public and made them more widely popular.

A few years later, in 1908, another American tea merchant was responsible for inadvertently inventing the teabag. New York dealer Thomas

Sullivan devised a stylish hand-sewn silk bag in which to send out samples of his teas to customers and they, finding the little bag very efficient and useful in a neat and tidy brewing operation, immediately demanded more of the same.

In the 1920s, prohibition, the motor car and the new independence enjoyed by women in the United States led to the opening of hundreds of new restaurants and tea-rooms right across the country. Tea-rooms with such names as The Blue Parrot Inn, Pine Tree Tea Room, Lady Baltimore Tea Room, Samovar, My Tea Wagon, Polly's Patio, The Cheshire Cat and many more sprang up in town centres, roadside resorts, village gardens, and in the lounges of hotels, inns and taverns – established and managed by women from all walks of life and from different backgrounds. Many bore scant resemblance to the stereotypical flowery parlours where little

THROUGH THE ALLEY
UP THE STAIRS AND
OVER THE ROOF AT
148 WEST FOURTH STREET
Greenwich Village   Phone Spring 7927

grey-haired old ladies nibbled on seed cakes and shortbreads. Some were bohemian garrets owned and staffed by artistic female entrepreneurs, some the stylish creations of adventurous, college-educated young women who favoured the modern look of the Arts & Crafts movement, some genteel and elegant establishments patronized by members of the upper classes, while others owed their success and charm to their Russian, Chinese, countryside, nursery rhyme or colonial theme. Sadly, just as happened in Britain, the fast-food boom of the 1950s led to the demise of the tea-room and by 1973 the *New York Times* was reporting that 'Ladies' tea-rooms are a dying breed'. Coffee bars and convenience food stores were starting to take over.

In the 1920s, the tea-room truly began to flourish in the United States.

Tea continued to be available generally to American consumers but most hotels, catering outlets, fast-food chains and restaurants offered very poor quality, badly brewed and poorly served tea. Today, as the result of a resurgence of interest that started on the East and West coasts but is now spreading throughout the United States, many discerning American consumers are demanding better quality tea, properly served.

The Renaissance of Tea

In China and Taiwan, tea companies have recognized the growing market around the world for tea and have gradually opened up their industry to allow easier trading, although many of the industry's secrets about the actual manufacture of the teas are still closely guarded.

In Japan, the exacting rituals of the traditional Green Tea Ceremony (see page 74) are still taught in evening classes around the country. For many Japanese, the ceremony is an important part of social etiquette and it remains an accepted and highly respected part of Japanese culture. The ceremony is regularly performed at special events and for foreign visitors. The everyday tea for most Japanese is green Sencha or Bancha, or roasted Houjicha. In the past ten to fifteen years, however, a growing taste for black tea drunk with milk in the British style has led to the general availability of black teas in supermarkets and department stores and the opening of many English-style tea-rooms where little sandwiches are carefully prepared with their crusts cut off, and scones are served with clotted cream and home-made preserves. Tea has been the central theme for several major Japanese events and trade fairs during the past ten years and many Japanese ladies are keen to learn more of the history and ceremony of tea-drinking in Britain.

In the United States a growing interest – and in some areas a real passion – for tea is being fuelled by the opening of excellent tea-rooms, the wider availability of good-quality teas, an understanding of tea's health benefits, and a genuine enjoyment of the countless different flavours and strengths that tea offers. What makes this new passion for tea so fascinating and rewarding is the way in which those involved are creating something new by adding their own twist to the story. No longer is every tea-room in the United States a nostalgic Victorian replica of what may once have existed in Britain. Instead, tea-rooms and tea retail shops are inspired and influenced by a fusion of European, Asian, Oriental and American tea styles. The selection of teas, the teawares used and sold, and the foods offered on the menu reflect the same awareness of the many different possibilities. Some tea-rooms are now attracting much younger customers who meet to exchange ideas, do homework, drink tea and relax, and many shops and tea venues also organize regular tastings and talks that help customers understand what tea is, where it is grown, how it is produced, why teas vary so much, different brewing methods, its health benefits and much more. Tea has also become the focus for education, medical and psychiatric specialists who are working with 'at risk' students at school, victims of crime, psychologically damaged patients and sick children. It seems that tea and its rituals help to create an atmosphere in which people feel

Teawares on display at Elmwood Inn Fine Teas, Kentucky

safe, calm, nurtured and protected and in which they can discuss their experiences and feelings in a way that is not possible for them elsewhere. This enthusiastic and powerful movement is being supported and encouraged by regular conferences, trade exhibitions, training courses, group trips to India, Sri Lanka, China and Taiwan, set up and run by a very well-organized and focused network of dedicated tea professionals.

In the UK, a small niche market for connoisseur teas is growing and a wider variety of teas is now on offer. The Tea Council's annual competitions to find Top Tea Place, Top London Afternoon Tea and Top Country House Hotel have also helped push up standards. Tea-rooms are busier than ever and their customers are showing a greater interest in, and becoming more discerning of, speciality single-source teas. As in the United States, an increased enthusiasm amongst the consuming public means a growing demand for a greater variety of teas, of higher quality, and for better standards of service. And as younger people begin to see tea as a stylish, healthy drink, tea is starting to take on more unusual guises — served in noodle bars that offer rare Chinese teas, in minimalist tea bars that offer quality brewed tea to take away as well as to drink on the premises, and in restaurants that offer a range of quality teas as an after-dinner alternative to coffee.

In many other parts of the world, people are discovering the benefits of tea and are seeking out information and suppliers as never before. In France, there are now more high-quality, elegant tea-rooms and tea salons than anywhere else in Europe and, as Glasgow was described in the 1880s as a veritable 'Tokyo of tearooms', so Paris is modern Europe's centre for tea. In Italy, health journalists, hoteliers, restaurateurs, event and wedding organizers, as well as tea-room owners and tea retailers, meet regularly to taste new teas, and to learn more about production, manufacture, brewing, serving and cooking with tea. In Germany, Spain, Holland, Belgium, Denmark, Sweden and Norway, and several countries of Eastern Europe, interest is also growing and retailers who have in the past sold modest amounts of tea are now finding that sales are increasing. In Moscow, five-star hotels are serving British-style 'afternoon tea'; in Georgia, tea-growers are exploring the possibility of opening a tea-room in Tbilisi to sell their hand-made teas and other quality teas from around the world; while in Hungary new tea retail stores are beginning to appear in malls and quality shopping areas. With the enlargement of the European Union and a greater stability and financial growth in Eastern Europe, sales in such countries as Poland, Latvia and Lithuania are also expected to grow.

Across the globe there is great excitement that the world of tea can offer such variety and choice: rich strong blacks from Africa and Sri Lanka; warm smooth malty teas from Assam; sappy first and second flush teas from Darjeeling; herby greens from Japan; sweet, velvety greens from China; rare hand-made teas from China and Taiwan; white teas with their silvery appearance and delicate fragrance; Puerh teas with their slightly earthy quality and accepted health benefits; and flavoured teas of all types.

Opposite ~ the Lanesborough Hotel, a classic setting for tea

Today, even people who once claimed not really to like tea are finding flavours to suit their palate.

So what is fuelling this renaissance? Three forces seem to be at work. Firstly, there is a genuine surprise at the number of options available and a realization that there is a tea to suit all tastes. Secondly, there is a widespread recognition that tea is a much healthier option than coffee, contains less caffeine and gives us many useful ingredients, such as polyphenols, which act as antioxidants to help protect our bodies from certain cancers and other degenerative age-related illnesses. It is also widely accepted today that tea offers an excellent alternative to harmful alcohol, pairs well with oriental foods, aids digestion, adds to essential daily fluid intake and, more importantly, refreshes and revives us. Thirdly, tea brings with it an amazing history, culture and spirituality that enriches the lives of all those who work with it, drink it and serve it to friends. Every tea-drinking nation has its own tea culture and rituals, all of which link back to the Zen origins of tea-drinking amongst Chinese and Japanese Buddhist priests. Through brewing and drinking, as through Zen, we can learn to focus on aspects of life that have real significance and importance – beautiful objects, carefully performed ceremonies that calm and centre us, harmonious communication with others, the sharing of memorable, peaceful moments, and the creation of quiet times away from the demanding pressures of everyday life.

The Tea Plant

The Tea Plant (*Thea sinensis*), classified by the famous Swedish botanist Linnaeus in 1753, is an evergreen plant of the Camellia genus and is also known as *Camellia sinensis*. The Chinese variety, *Camellia sinensis sinensis*, is sub-divided into two other main subspecies known as *Camellia sinensis assamica*, the plant that grows as a native of India's north-eastern province of Assam, and *Camellia sinensis subspecies lasiocalyx*, the Cambodian variety.

The Camellia sinensis *flower*

The plant grows as an evergreen shrub or tree that produces delicate little flowers with five or seven white or creamy-white petals and bright sunshine-yellow stamens, and whose sharply serrated leaves are thick and shiny. The bitter-tasting fruit is the size of a hazelnut and contains one to three seeds.

The Chinese bush generally grows to a maximum height of 5 metres (15 feet) and has several closely clumped stems, but ancient tea trees exist in China that reach heights of over 30 metres (100 feet), the oldest still growing in the Xishuangbanna region of Yunnan Province. The *Camellia sinensis* does not mind cold climates and grows well in China, Tibet, Japan and other high tea-growing regions of the world such as Taiwan and the upper slopes of the Darjeeling plantations in India. The leaves grow to roughly 5 centimetres (2 inches) in length and the bushes can go on producing good tea for up to a hundred years.

The *Camellia sinensis assamica* is a tree rather than a bush, growing with a central trunk and reaching heights of 14–18 metres (45–60 feet). If allowed to grow freely, the leaves can grow to between 15–35 centimetres (6–14 inches) in length. The Assam variety loves hot and humid conditions and goes on producing for approximately forty years. There are five main types of *Camellia sinensis assamica* – the hardy Burma and Manipuri varieties, the Lushai variety, a tender-leafed variety and a dark-leafed Assam type. All give a darker, fuller-flavoured tea than the Chinese bushes.

The Cambodian variety is also considered to be a tree rather than a bush and grows with a single trunk to heights of roughly 4.5 metres (15 feet). It is generally only used in creating hybrids.

Today tea bushes and trees are grown around the globe in areas close to the equator where the tropical conditions suit the plant best. The most suitable climates offer temperatures ranging from 50–85°C (120–180°F), rainfall of between 200 and 230 centimetres (80 and 90 inches) a year, and elevations of between 300 and 2,100 metres (1,000 and 7,000 feet) above sea level. The best plantations are at altitudes of between 1,200 and 1,800 metres (4,000 and 6,000 feet), where mist and cloud help protect the plants from too much direct sunlight and cooler air allows the delicate new buds and leaves to develop and grow more slowly, thus giving more flavour. The term 'high-grown' refers to teas cultivated above 1,200 metres (4,000 feet), 'mid-grown' to teas grown between 600 and 1,200 metres (2,000 and 4,000 feet), and 'low-grown' to those cultivated below 600 metres (2,000 feet).

The plant's shallow root system lies only a metre or so below the surface and is therefore vulnerable to droughts and floods. Soil that is too dry or that drains too quickly will cause the bush to quickly wilt and stop producing new leaf buds. Too much rain and the roots will be drowned. So good drainage and suitable acid soil (clay, peat and sand are all good) are essential to successful cultivation.

Cultivating the Plant

Today, rather than growing new bushes from seed, planters produce new stock from cuttings and cloned leaves taken from suitable 'mother' plants. The parent bushes are carefully selected for their ability to grow vigorously, give a high yield, withstand the onslaught of pests, resist drought and flooding, and produce high-quality leaf with plenty of white hairy down on the underside. Tea Research Centres all over the tea-growing world have been working intensively for over a decade to develop ways of evaluating potential clonal stock and selecting faster-growing, higher-yielding plants. This allows farmers to develop plantations more efficiently and significantly raise profit margins.

The young plants are carefully tended in the nursery for a period varying from 6 to 20 months, depending on the climate, and are then planted out into the tea garden in a space measuring between 1 and 1½ square metres (12 and 16 square feet). Planting follows the natural contours of the landscape and the land is sometimes specially terraced to help eliminate soil erosion. The new plants are left unplucked and unpruned for two years until they reach a height of roughly 1½–2 metres (5–6 feet). They are then regularly pruned to keep them to a height of just under a metre and the bushes are encouraged to spread sideways and fill across to the neighbouring bushes. The surface created is referred to as the 'plucking table' and the new leaves that appear on the top are ready to be included in the manufacture of tea after they have spent three years at lower altitudes and five at high elevations. In areas where very hot direct sunshine threatens the health and growth of the plants, shade trees are planted to offer some protection.

In areas where weather conditions remain constant throughout the year, such as Kenya, the plant goes on growing without rest, while in regions where the seasons change, such as north-eastern India and China, there is a dormant period during which the bushes do not grow. Plucking takes place as the bushes 'flush' and push out new leaf shoots. In hot, steady climates, the plants flush regularly while in cooler, seasonal regions picking goes on from early spring to late autumn. In some seasonal areas (for example in Darjeeling), the first flush is considered to give the best, most fragrant teas. These teas develop slowly in the cooler spring sunshine and enjoy the concentrated essence of the bush after the winter dormancy. But in other parts of the world, for example in Assam, it is the second flush that wins prizes and fetches higher prices.

For the finest teas, the pickers 'fine pluck' the new shoots by taking only the first two new leaves and one new bud. The delicate new shoots are grasped lightly between the tip of the thumb and the tip of the middle finger and then carefully broken off with a quick downward movement. The tender young shoots are then thrown over the shoulder into baskets or bags carried on the pickers' backs. In Darjeeling, where the leaves are small, roughly 22,000 new shoots are needed to give just one kilo of made tea whereas in Assam, where the leaves are bigger, roughly 10,000 shoots will produce one kilo of made tea.

A tea-picker at work on a Sri Lankan plantation.

Fine-plucking - the newest, tenderest leaves are selected by highly skilled pickers.

Pickers start work early in the morning while the dew is still on the bushes so that they can get the youngest, most tender, new growth and meet the targets set by quantity requirements.

The alternative to fine plucking is medium and coarse plucking. These give a larger quantity and weight of leaf but a lower quality of tea. With medium plucking, three leaves and a bud are snapped off, while coarse plucking includes all shoots that have two leaves and a bud, three leaves and a bud and four leaves and a bud. The climate and location affect how often the bushes are plucked. In Kenya, the bushes push out new shoots throughout the year and are plucked every 7–14 days. In Sri Lanka, new shoots are gathered every 7 days in wet weather and every 10 days in dry. As the pickers work through the field or plantation, they also break off any coarse leaf and dormant shoots and throw them to the ground.

In some parts of the world, labour is either too expensive or simply not available for tea-picking and bushes must be harvested mechanically. Over the past few years, researchers have developed shears that are used to clip the tea shoots off in much the same way as would hedge clippers – hand-held machinery that is manoeuvred by two workers over the plucking table. Alternatively, pluckers use large tractor-like machines that trundle between the rows of bushes, cutting off any top growth. Because machines can never be as discerning as human pickers, machine-harvested tea inevitably contains stalk and older, coarser leaves as well as fresh growth. This method consequently results in a poorer-quality tea.

Care of the Bushes

Each plantation or field of bushes is regularly pruned to remove any dead wood, to encourage vigorous growth and to maintain the even and constant height of the plucking table. While pruning is taking place, plantation managers also take the opportunity of cleaning drains and cutting new drainage channels into the soil.

Weed control is a crucial part of plantation husbandry and represents the second highest cost in tea cultivation after plucking. Young tea plants are more sensitive to the activity of weeds than mature plants and so need more intensive care. In some cases, hand-weeding and the use of hoes, sickles and forks keep the plants free from the predatory growth of unwanted plants, but the most widespread and efficient form of control is through the carefully controlled application of relevant herbicides.

The most common diseases affecting tea bushes are various root diseases, which can kill the plants, cause them to produce discoloured leaf or lead to the development of fungal growth on the bushes; stem and branch diseases, which can kill off individual branches and cause the growth of fungus; leaf diseases, which can cause discoloration and spotting on the leaves; and a lack of certain minerals in the soil, which can cause bushes to produce distorted leaves, discoloured flush, buds that do not develop or that die off, or leaves that are brittle or drop prematurely. All of these are treated with specific chemical and mineral applications to the soil or by removing the affected bushes and infilling with new stock. The plants can equally be damaged by insects, mites and rodents and these are dealt with by pesticides and population control.

The soil is enriched naturally by the application of manure, compost and mulched material gathered during pruning.

Tea Types and Manufacture

Across the globe, more than 3,000 different teas are made from different varieties of the *Camellia sinensis*. As with the production of wine, the character, colour and flavour of each tea when it is brewed and served are determined by a long list of variable factors – location of the plantation, altitude, climate, seasonal changes, cultivation methods, plucking methods, how the leaf is processed, what happens to the leaf at the end of the manufacturing process, and the way in which the tea is eventually brewed. Levels of caffeine (in the past also known as theine) vary in different teas. This is thought to depend on the age of the leaf when it is picked, its location on the stem, the length of oxidation time, the size of the tea leaves brewed and the quantity of leaf used to make the brew.

WHITE TEA

White tea is named after the tiny white or silver hairs that cover the bud as it develops at the tip of each tea shoot. Originally only made in China from two varieties of the tea plant (Shui Hsien or Water Sprite, and Dai Bai or Big White), white teas are now being produced in other parts of the world. The teas are usually made from just the unopened bud, gathered before it can start to unfurl, although some white teas (including Bai Mudan) also include a few very new leaves that have opened slightly. The size of the buds varies and whereas some are made from sturdy buds that can measure up to an inch in length, others are smaller, thinner and more wiry in appearance. Once the brand new buds have been carefully gathered, they are de-enzymed by steaming, sometimes shaped by hand, and then dried. When brewed they give a very pale, champagne-coloured liquor that has a very light, soft, sweet, velvety flavour. The caffeine content of such teas is minimal and the lowest of all tea types.

Yellow teas are China's rarest. Similar to white teas, they are made from the skilfully picked new buds which are then piled and left so that the heat generated from the natural oxidation process dries them out and prevents any further decomposition. When infused, the buds give a pale yellowy-green liquor that has a delicate sweetness. There is more caffeine in the infusion than in the brew from most green teas.

GREEN TEA

Green teas are generally described as 'unoxidized' or 'unfermented' teas and no chemical change occurs during their manufacture. Processing differs from country to country but the basic manufacture involves withering, to allow some of the water content to evaporate, or steaming, to de-enzyme the leaf. To wither the leaves, as soon as they are brought to the factory they are spread out on cool cement floors or rattan sacking in open sunshine or warm rooms for one or two hours, depending on the ambient temperature. Then comes a series of rollings and firings. In China, the leaf is alternately rolled by hand and fired, giving each tea its own characteristic shape – the tiny pellets of Gunpowder, the curved eyebrow shape of Chun Mee, or the tightly wound spirals of Biluochun. Some mechanization has been introduced into Chinese tea production but the best quality, most highly prized teas are all hand-made and the skills involved are passed on from one generation to the next. In Japan, the entire process is mechanized and the leaves are first steamed on a rapidly moving conveyor belt to make them soft and supple, then cooled and repeatedly rolled, pressed, sorted, polished and dried before being cooled again and packed at the end of the production line. At the end of the process, only 3%–6% moisture remains in the leaf.

OOLONG TEA

Oolong teas, known as half- or semi-oxidized, or half- or semi-fermented, teas are traditionally manufactured in China and Taiwan, but other countries are now producing them too. In order to give a rich flavour, fresh shoots with one new bud and three leaves are gathered as they reach their peak on the bush and are immediately processed. First the leaves are wilted in warm air, then they are shaken in bamboo baskets so that the edges of the leaves become lightly bruised. This means that there will be a certain amount of oxidation during the subsequent processing. The parts of the leaf that have not been bruised remain unchanged while the natural juices in the parts of the leaf that have been broken by the shaking are released and react with oxygen in the air, darkening those parts of the leaf and causing a fuller, richer flavour to develop. The shaking and oxidation processes are continued alternately for a number of hours until they are 70% green and 30% red-brown and, to stop further oxidation, the leaves are then dried over charcoal-fired stoves. In Taiwan, the bruising is carried out by wrapping the wilted leaves inside a white cloth and rolling the ball on a special machine. The cloth is then unwrapped and the leaves allowed to oxidize for a short time before being wrapped and rolled several more times. After drying, oolong teas are graded by a skilled tea master who judges the different leaves by their appearance, flavour and character.

When steeped in boiling water, oolong teas give a reddish-brown, clear infusion that often has a fruity or perfumed aroma and a smooth but complex often peach or apricot flavour. Oolong teas contain more caffeine than green teas but less than black teas.

Bao Zhing (Pouchong) teas are a type of oolong but because of a shorter oxidation time they have a much greener appearance. They give a light, clean-tasting infusion that is sweet and fresh.

BLACK TEA

For black tea, methods of manufacture and the varieties produced vary enormously from country to country and from region to region, but the process always involves four basic stages – withering, rolling, oxidation (fermenting) and firing (drying). The two major processing methods are 'orthodox' and 'CTC'. The traditional orthodox method is still used in China, Taiwan, India, Sri Lanka, Indonesia and elsewhere, and tends to treat the leaf with more respect that the modern CTC method. For orthodox teas, the leaves (78–80% water when picked) are spread out in warm air and allowed to wither (to a water content of 30–40%) until soft enough to be rolled without breaking the surface of the leaf. The yellow-green leaf is then rolled in a special rolling machine that presses and twists the leaves, breaking the cells inside them and releasing the natural juices and chemicals that will start the oxidation process. The number of rolls varies from two to four, sometimes with additional rolls in a rotorvane machine to maximize production of the smaller broken grades.

After rolling, the leaf is broken up and spread out in thin layers in cool humid air and left to oxidize for 3–4 hours, depending on the conditions and temperature. The leaf now begins to develop its recognizable aroma and flavour, becomes darker in colour and develops caffeine and tea chemicals such as theaflavin. To arrest the oxidation, the tea is finally fed into large automatic dryers inside which it is carried along on conveyor belts and where hot air at a temperature of 115–120°C (240–250°F) reduces the moisture content of the tea to just 2–3%.

The CTC (Cut, Tear and Curl) method of manufacture is widely used in major tea-producing countries to give a small-leafed tea that brews more quickly and yields a strong liquor – characteristics that are essential for the production of teabag blends. This process was de-

From top ~ withering, rolling, oxidizing

veloped in the 1950s when the teabag was becoming more popular. To produce such teas, the leaf is withered in the same way as for orthodox teas but, instead of being rolled, it is macerated by the rollers of a CTC machine which rotate at different speeds, or in a Lawrie Tea Processor (LTP) rotating hammer-mill leaf disintegrator, which tears and breaks the leaf into tiny particles. The remaining oxidation and drying stages of the process are the same as for orthodox black teas.

PUERH TEA

Known only in China for centuries, Puerh tea is now recognized to have numerous positive health benefits and is consequently becoming more and more popular throughout the world. Its earthy, matured flavour is an acquired taste but as more people discover it and become familiar with its unusual character, it is finding new markets everywhere. It is thought to be excellent for the digestion and to ease stomach upsets. It is thought also to help reduce cholesterol in the blood and to help those on a diet lose weight more easily.

Puerh teas all come from Yunnan Province in south-west China and are made from a large-leafed variety of the *Camellia sinensis* that grows in the area. The Yunnan soil and climate produce a tea that has a rich, earthy flavour and which is matured or aged to an elemental, slightly 'mouldy' character by a special process that has been developed over the centuries. Puerh teas are classified into two types – Black Process Puerh and Green Process Puerh. The process for making Black Puerhs involves a 'pile-fermentation' during which the leaves ferment and change from green to a darker, brown leaf before being dried. This fermentation can last for up to three months, depending on the local conditions. Green Puerhs are made by steaming the leaves before drying them. The teas are then aged for up to 30 years and are sold loose or in a variety of compressed forms. Puerh teas are not actually made in the town of Puerh but in other areas of Yunnan Province. The name is used because the town has always been the centre for the marketing of these special aged teas.

COMPRESSED TEA

More than one thousand years ago in China, during the days of the Tang

Dynasty (AD618–906), tea producers started compressing processed tea leaves into cakes or bricks in order to conserve the leaf and make it easier to transport. Many compressed teas that are available today actually consist of Puerh tea, though others are made from normal green or black teas. The shapes of compressed teas vary from neat little bowls to flat circles or triangles, bowls shaped like birds' nests, globes in the

Compressing tea into 'bricks' makes it easier to transport.

form of a melon, tiny discs or balls and rectangular or square slabs. Some are wrapped in bamboo or dried banana leaves; others are packed inside grasses or paper. Some are packed singly, others in a stack of four or more cakes. To brew compressed teas, the required amount is flaked or broken off with the fingers or a knife blade and the crumbled tea is then steeped in hot water for 1 to 5 minutes. The longer the tea is steeped, the darker the colour of the liquor and the stronger the flavour. Black compressed Puerh tea can be steeped two or three times. Green Puerh can be re-steeped several times.

FLAVOURED TEA

Any type of tea – white, green, oolong or black – may be scented or flavoured with flowers, fruits, spices or herbs. The additional flavourings are blended with the leaf at the end of the manufac-turing process in the form of essential oils, pieces of dried fruit or spice, flower petals, or lit-tle pellets of flavouring that gradually release their scent into the tea. Once flavoured, the teas are then packed as teabags or loose leaf.

Green tea flavoured with vanilla and orange

One of the best known flavoured teas is Earl Grey, which is made by blending black or green tea with the essential oil of bergamot.

The Production of Tea

This Chinese citrus fruit gives the tea a refreshing orangy-lemon flavour. Other flavoured teas popular around the world are Jasmine, made by allowing the heady perfume of fresh jasmine flowers to permeate the tea; Rose Petal, which has the deliciously sweet scent of pink roses; and mint, which is usually made with China Gunpowder and pieces of dried mint leaf. The possibilities are endless and today's flavoured teas range from such simple mixtures as lemon tea to complex blends that include several different flowers and exotic spices.

Some teas have their own natural flavouring, acquired from the plants amongst which they grow. One particular variety of Orchid tea from China, for example, absorbs the rich sweetness of the orchids that grow wild in the tea garden. And tea bushes that grow adjacent to fruit trees will naturally take on a hint of the scent given off by the blossoms and the fruit.

Sencha flavoured with cherry blossom

Flavoured teas should not be confused with herbal infusions that are made from plants other than the *Camellia sinensis* (the tea plant). Many herbs and flowers, for example camomile, mint, rosehip and hibiscus, are used to give soothing, beneficial brews but if the leaves of the tea plant are not included, neither the dried product nor the liquor should be referred to as 'tea'. The correct name is 'infusion', 'herbal' or 'tisane'. Packaging should make it clear to consumers what is actually inside the packet – just tea, tea mixed with flavourings, or just herbs, flowers, spices and fruits.

DECAFFEINATED TEA

It is the caffeine that gives tea its ability to refresh us, increase our ability to concentrate and keep us going through the day. Caffeine is a stimulant that helps increase the speed of our reactions, makes us more alert, stimulates the digestive system and the activity of the kidneys and so helps to clean the body of unwanted toxins. There is an important difference in the way in which we absorb the caffeine in coffee and the caffeine in tea.

When we drink coffee, the caffeine content goes instantly into our circulatory system, jolting us into wakefulness, causing the pulse to beat faster and the blood to pump more vigorously around our bodies. When we drink tea, the caffeine is released much more slowly (because of the controlling effects of the other ingredients in the tea) and takes 15 to 20 minutes to be absorbed. So, instead of being released into the bloodstream, the caffeine goes more gently into our central nervous system and helps to heighten our senses and increase our wakefulness. The effects of the caffeine in tea are therefore felt more slowly, stay with us for longer and tail off more gradually than with coffee. Tea really is a much more efficient 'pick-me-up'.

Caffeine is a mild cardiac stimulant and a mild diuretic and can cause problems for people with heart or kidney conditions. For those who cannot or do not wish to take caffeine into their bodies, decaffeinated tea is readily available, although the quality and flavour vary considerably, depending on the decaffeination process. Three different methods are used to remove the caffeine – carbon dioxide, methylene chloride and ethyl acetate.

Carbon dioxide is an organic solvent that is cheap to use, easy to remove from the tea after decaffeination, and harmless in small quantities. CO_2 is pumped into a chamber containing tea and it bubbles through the tea solution to remove the caffeine. The CO_2 is then removed from the chamber, separated from the caffeine and reintroduced into the chamber to absorb more caffeine. This process is repeated several times. The benefits of this method are that no chemical residue is left in the tea and the flavour and tea compounds are relatively unharmed.

Methylene chloride is the most popular and most widely used agent to extract caffeine from tea and is easily removed from the tea after decaffeination. It is approved by the American food standards body, the FDA (the Food and Drug Administration section of the US Department of Health and Human Services). To decaffeinate tea, the methylene chloride is applied either directly or indirectly to the tea. During the 'direct' method, the methylene chloride is applied to wet tea leaves and then removed with the caffeine. The decaffeinated leaves are then washed and dried. During the 'indirect' method (whereby the methylene chloride never comes into contact with the tea itself), the tea is first soaked in water to extract the caffeine (and other tea ingredients such as polyphenols and oils that give the tea its flavour and health benefits). The caffeine and water are then mixed with methylene chloride and heated to evaporate the caffeine and methylene chloride, leaving water and tea extracts which are then reintroduced to the tea.

Ethyl acetate is classed as a natural element that is found in tea, coffee, wine and bananas and is used in flavour enhancers for ice-creams, confectionery, cakes and perfumes. Because it occurs naturally, some people consider it to be the best agent for decaffeination and the FDA considers it to be GRAS (Generally Regarded as Safe). However, during the decaffeination process, it extracts other components as well as the caffeine and is difficult to remove from the decaffeinated tea.

ORGANIC TEA

The cultivation of any food product under organic rules is extremely rigidly controlled by various international bodies. No chemical fertilizers, pesticides, herbicides or other chemical additives of any kind may be used anywhere on the plantation and producers must rely totally on natural methods of pest and insect control, and on sprays, mulches and fertilizers that are made from dung, natural compost and other organic matter. Companies involved in organic production are concerned with the long-term health of our planet and organic tea plantations try to give back to the earth as well as take out. By using natural pest control (for example by reintroducing ladybirds and other harmless pest-eating insects such as aphids), they aim to protect rather than harm the environment while at the same time producing tea that is totally free of chemical additives.

Organic production is labour intensive and therefore expensive but as more people around the globe begin to share the organic producers' concerns, an extensive range of organic tea products is becoming widely available through tea retailers and supermarkets. Some planters have taken organic production one step further and work in harmony with the universe to produce what is called 'bio-dynamic' tea. This means that the seasons, the weather, the waxing and waning of the moon and the interaction and interdependency of different species of insects, birds and animals are all taken into consideration when planting, pruning and all the other aspects of tea cultivation are being planned and implemented.

Even without organic production methods, tea is actually an incredibly clean product whose cultivation and production are tightly controlled by strict EU and US rules of health and public safety. Yet the number of people who take into consideration the long-term health and viability of the planet when buying everyday commodities, and who care about and appreciate the fine quality and flavour of organic products, is now considerable, and continues to grow. For them, a wide range of organic teas is now available from Africa, Sri Lanka, India, China and Japan.

INSTANT TEA

Although manufacturers have been working for a number of years to produce an instant tea that competes successfully with instant coffee, none of the products available offers a flavour that resembles the true flavour of tea. Real tea connoisseurs consider instant tea to be an anathema and would never brew tea in this way. The idea of spooning a measure of dry granules or powder into a mug or cup and dissolving it in boiling water has nothing whatsoever to do with the brewing of a good cup of tea. The traditional brewing ceremonies in different cultures around the world – involving loose-leaf tea, a measuring spoon, a brewing vessel and beautiful cups or bowls from which to drink – are as much about the ritual as they are about preparing the drink and should never be abandoned for the sake of saving a few minutes. That time gained is time lost in terms of the calming influence and spiritual rewards of a traditional tea ritual.

Instant tea is manufactured by infusing tea leaves in water to extract flavour, caffeine and other tea components. The leaf and the brew are then separated, the leaf is discarded, and the solution is further treated to obtain a solid dry product. This is achieved by first heating the solution to evaporate the water content, then freezing the solution so that ice particles can be separated out, and finally filtering the solution through special membranes which hold back the solids but allow the water to pass through. After separation, the solids are freeze-dried or spray-dried and the resulting powder or granules are carefully packed in air-tight or vacuum packs. Whereas loose-leaf tea is rarely packed into glass jars, instant tea is almost always packed in this way.

Some companies are now producing instant teas flavoured with fruits and flowers, as has long been the practice with loose teas. Attempts are being made to create a finished product that is more attractive in terms of aroma, taste and colour, and packaging is beginning to reflect a more modern and stylish approach, in an effort to lure tea-drinkers away from traditionally brewed tea.

READY-TO-DRINK TEA

For many years in Japan, 'ready-to-drink' (RTD) teas have been available from machines on street corners and in supermarkets. The range offers hot or cold, green or black, with milk or without, sweetened or without sugar, tea from Japan or from Darjeeling and Assam. It is very common to see people feeding coins into one of these machines in order to obtain the right tea for the occasion or the weather.

The market for such RTD teas has been growing in the West since the early 1990s when the American tea industry launched the first bottled and

'Ready-to-drink' teas on sale in Japan

canned, still and carbonated, tea-flavoured drinks. To capture the largest possible share of the market and to give new products the benefit of a major advertising drive, tea companies joined forces with soft drink and cola manufacturers to create a range of tea-based, fruit-flavoured conven-ience drinks. These were marketed through supermarkets, convenience stores and small retail shops in competition with colas and other similar drinks. Since then, many new varieties have appeared, some over-sweet-ened, some with no sugar at all, some based on black tea, others using Japanese and Chinese green tea extracts, some with herb, spice and fruit flavourings, some with nothing but the tea and water in the bottle. The amount of tea in any of these drinks is minimal but the best of the selec-tion do offer a much more appealing and satisfying drink than some of the more familiar cold canned and bottled drinks that contain far too much sugar, are way too gassy and never seem to quench one's thirst.

By purchasing 'fairly traded' goods, consumers aim to help ensure that workers in producing countries are not exploited but receive a share in the profitability of the company they work for. Tea has always been a very ethical industry and workers in most countries are well paid (in relative terms, according to average pay in the country in which they live and work). Plantations are generally run as small communities where provision of good housing and water, crèches, schools, clinics and hospitals is a prime concern of the plantation owners. However, Fair Trade attempts to redress the imbalance between the wages of workers in the developing countries and the profits made by major companies in the consuming countries. Products are sold through the normal channels of supermarkets, smaller retail outlets, websites and mail order catalogues. A percentage of the profits is paid back to the producing estates and goes towards improving the quality of life for the workers through pension schemes, alternative training programmes, welfare and medical pro-grammes, and to improving the environment through important initiatives such as the planting of trees to stop soil erosion and landslides. Fair Trade teas are now available from various approved sources in China, India, Sri Lanka, Nepal, Tanzania, Uganda, Zimbabwe, Kenya and Vietnam.

The Ethical Tea Partnership

In the UK, the Ethical Tea Partnership, set up in 1997 under its original name of the Tea Sourcing Partnership by a group of British tea-packing companies, works with similar objectives to Fair Trade but in a slightly different way. The ETP seeks to monitor conditions on tea estates in the seven countries whose teas are most commonly drunk in Britain – Kenya, Malawi, Sri Lanka, India, Indonesia, Tanzania and Zimbabwe – because its members believe that they have a shared responsibility for the social and ethical conditions involved in tea production, packing and supply. The organization seeks to guarantee that member companies only buy their tea from ethical producers who comply with local legislation and union agree-ments concerning terms and conditions of employment, health and safety, maternity and housing on the estates, as well as education and basic rights.

The Production of Tea

When made tea emerges from drying machines at the end of the manufacturing process, it consists of a mixture of different-sized pieces of leaf. For successful brewing, these pieces must be sorted into different grades (or sizes), since different-sized particles brew at different rates. If the particles are of mixed sizes, the tea will brew unevenly. So, once the tea has been dried, it is either sorted by hand or passed through sifters with graduated mesh sizes to separate the particles. The different sizes are then classified according to size, type and appearance. Systems of classification vary from country to country.

In China, teas are named by region, the time of year when the tea was picked, the method of manufacture, the leaf type used, or the legend behind the origination of the tea. For example, Chun Mee means Precious Eyebrows, from the gently curved shape of the dried green leaves; Jiuqu

Grades of Puerh tea

Wulong means Nine-Bend Stream Black Dragon (Jiuqu means Nine-Bend Stream and Wulong or Oolong translates as Black Dragon); and Rose Congou is black tea skilfully made by hand (Congou, like kung fu, comes from the Chinese word 'gongfu' and has to do with skill, as in Chinese martial arts), and blended with dried pink rose petals before packaging.

In India, Sri Lanka and other traditional producing countries where the orthodox method of manufacture for black teas is still used, grading terms divide the leaf into 'leaf' grades and 'broken leaf' grades. Broken leaf grades refer to what is left after the leaf grades have been sifted out.

In the African continent and in other countries that manufacture black tea for use in teabags by the CTC method (see page 39), a further system of grading terminology has developed in order to differentiate the much smaller grainy particles.

Teas are divided into the following categories (black teas only):

FLOWERY ORANGE PEKOE (FOP)

This denotes tea made from the end bud and first two leaves of each new shoot and the term refers to the largest leaves. FOP contains fine, tender, young leaves that have been rolled with a good balance of correct 'tip' (the delicate end pieces of the leaf buds), which guarantees quality. The word 'pekoe' derives from the Chinese word *pek-ho* or *baihao*, and refers to the covering of tiny silvery hairs on the underside of the leaves of certain types of the tea bush. Orange comes, we think, from Holland's 'House of Orange', the royal family of the first European country to import and re-export tea and thus a name connected with the very best quality.

TGFOP

GOLDEN FLOWERY ORANGE PEKOE (GFOP)

This is FOP with 'golden tips' – the very end of the golden yellow leaf buds.

TIPPY GOLDEN FLOWERY ORANGE PEKOE (TGFOP) [*Right*]

This is FOP with a large proportion of golden tips.

FINEST TIPPY GOLDEN FLOWERY ORANGE PEKOE (FTGFOP)

This is exceptionally high-quality FOP.

SPECIAL FINEST TIPPY GOLDEN FLOWERY ORANGE PEKOE (SFTGFOP)
[*Right*]
This is the very best FOP.

ORANGE PEKOE (OP) [*Left*]
Contains long pointed leaves that are larger than FOP and have been harvested when the end buds are opening into leaves. Seldom contains 'tips'.

PEKOE (P)
This consists of shorter, coarser leaves than OP.

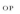

OP

FLOWERY PEKOE (FP)
Flowery Pekoe consists of leaves that have been
rolled lengthwise and the pieces are shorter and
coarser than OP.

PEKOE SOUCHONG (PS)
This consists of shorter, coarser leaves than Pekoe.

SFTGFOP

SOUCHONG (S)
The word 'souchong' means 'sub-variety' in Chinese, a term associated with large leaves that have been rolled lengthwise to produce ragged, coarse pieces. Souchong is often used for smoked teas from China and Taiwan.

Broken Leaf Grades are divided into the following categories:

Golden Flowery Broken Orange Pekoe (GFBOP)
Golden Broken Orange Pekoe (GBOP)
Tippy Golden Broken Orange Pekoe (TGBOP) [*Below*]
Tippy Flowery Broken Orange Pekoe (TFBOP)
Tippy Golden Flowery Broken Orange Pekoe (TGFBOP)
Flowery Broken Orange Pekoe (FBOP)
Broken Orange Pekoe (BOP)
Broken Pekoe Souchong (BPS)

TGBOP

Fannings

Fannings (also referred to as Fines or Dusts) are made up of the finest siftings left after the larger whole leaf and broken leaf particles have been removed. They are useful in blends for teabags, which require a quick brewing tea. The number 1 is also added to the broken leaf grades to denote the best quality (eg PF 1, Dust 1). Dusts and Fannings are further categorized as:

Orange Fannings (OF)
Broken Orange Pekoe Fannings (BOPF) [*Right*]
Pekoe Fannings (PF)
Broken Pekoe Fannings (BPF)
Pekoe Dust (PD)

BOPF

CTC teas are generally categorized as follows:

Broken Orange Pekoe (BOP)
Broken Pekoe (BP)
Broken Pekoe 1 or 2
Fannings (F) or (FNGS)
Pekoe Dust (PD)
Dust (D)
Dust 2 (D2)
Red Dust (RD) [*Below right*]
Broken Mixed Fannings (BMF)

RD

Just like wine connoisseurs, tea connoisseurs enjoy the fact that the flavour and quality of different teas vary from year to year and from season to season because of inevitable changes in the weather or slight differences in the manufacturing process. They take pleasure in comparing a First Flush Darjeeling from, for example, Margaret's Hope Estate to a First Flush Darjeeling from Castleton, or a Second Flush Assam from Harmutty in 2004 to a Second Flush from Harmutty in 2005.

Yet some tea-drinkers prefer to know that each time they buy a particular tea, for example, English Breakfast or Earl Grey, Ceylon Blend or Darjeeling, it will always taste the same and give the same strength and flavour. It is for this reason that tea blenders and packers create blends to suit their customers. To do this they must taste hundreds of samples of different teas every day in order to find the mix of up to 35 different teas that will give that standard flavour. The blenders taste teas from different estates, different regions and different seasons and then create a recipe using the selected teas. It's a little like wine-blending or perfumery in that the ingredients vary in number and range but the final result must always be the same.

In order to assess the different teas, tea tasters prepare the teas by a strict set of rules. The dry leaf teas are set out in their containers in a long row on the tasting bench. A specific weight of each tea is then carefully measured into a special lidded brewing mug and boiling water for black teas, or slightly cooler water for green teas, is poured on. A timer is set and when the leaves have steeped for 5 – 6 minutes (sometimes shorter for certain green teas) the lidded mugs are tipped on their side in a tasting bowl and the serration in the lip of the mug allows the tea to run into the bowl. The wet leaves are knocked out onto the upturned lid of the mug and set close to the tasting bowl. The taster then uses a rounded spoon to slurp some of the tea sharply into the mouth so that it hits the taste buds. The liquor is rolled around the mouth to assess the full flavour before being spat out into a mobile spittoon that trundles along beside the work bench. When assessing the tea's quality and value, the taster takes

Right ~
setting out the
tasting bench

into consideration the appearance of the dry leaf, the appearance and smell of the wet leaf, and the appearance, taste and aroma of the liquor.

Once the right recipe for a particular blend has been decided, the necessary teas are loaded into large, funnel-shaped containers (hoppers) which feed a blending drum where the teas are mixed thoroughly together. The blend is then packed in the usual way.

Classic Blends

Certain blends have developed over the centuries according to the preference of individual tea-drinking nationalities. The British have always liked a robust strong tea to wake them up in the morning and so English Breakfast blends have traditionally been made up of teas that give a rich flavour and a good, dark coppery colour. To create such a mixture, blenders choose from teas they know to have the appropriate characteristics.

ENGLISH BREAKFAST

In Britain, this is almost always made up of a blend of teas from Assam, for its warm malty smoothness, Sri Lanka, for its brisk golden quality, and Kenya, for its strength and depth of flavour and colour. Some American companies use China Keemun teas exclusively as the base for their English Breakfast blends and the choice of teas depends very much on the personal preferences of individual blenders.

IRISH BREAKFAST

The Irish like their tea very strong and dark and the blend is similar to English Breakfast but usually includes a greater proportion of Kenya tea and sometimes black teas from Indonesia.

INDIAN BREAKFAST

Usually a blend of Darjeeling and Assam, or Assam and Nilgiri, or a mixture of teas from all three areas. These blends tend to be lighter than English Breakfast blends and include the distinctive character of fruity, slightly astringent Darjeelings.

EARL GREY

Probably the most popular and well-known flavoured blend in the world, this is traditionally a blend of China black tea and essential oil of bergamot. Some tea companies today offer green, oolong and decaffeinated Earl Grey as well as black. Several stories, all of which relate to Earl Grey who was British prime minister from 1830 to 1834, have developed over the years to explain the origin of this famous tea, but it is impossible to know if any of them are true. One tale tells how a British diplomat, while on a mission to China during Earl Grey's premiership,

saved the life of a mandarin and was given the recipe to take home to the prime minister as a symbol of gratitude. Another tells that it was the Earl himself who saved the Chinese nobleman. Yet another features the tea as a gift presented to Earl Grey at the end of a successful diplomatic visit to China. However, as far as we know, although the Chinese have flavoured their tea with many different extra ingredients over the centuries, bergamot is never mentioned as one of them and such colourful legends may simply have been an intelligent marketing ploy.

Earl Grey, the British prime minister who gave the famous blend its name

RUSSIAN CARAVAN

A blend of black teas from China that often has a slightly smoky flavour. This blend attempts to recreate the taste of the teas that were transported back to Moscow from the Chinese border after furs had been traded for tea. Since the journey by camel caravan was long and slow, the group of traders would stop for the night and light campfires and it is said that the tea absorbed a certain smokiness from the fires. Today's blends often include just a hint of Lapsang Souchong.

AFTERNOON BLEND

Usually a blend of black teas from Sri Lanka and India but sometimes with added flavourings such as jasmine or bergamot. Some tea-blending companies prefer to create a very light tea for the afternoon and base the blend on Darjeeling or Chinese and Taiwanese teas.

Own Blends

Blends can easily be created to suit different tastes, different times of the day and different foods. Successful blending is usually the result of experimentation and tasting, trial and error. Some people like to add a hint of Earl Grey to a favourite Ceylon or Assam, others like the smokiness of Lapsang Souchong added to their English Breakfast blend.

Teas can also be flavoured at home by the addition of a few dried flower petals, pieces of spice or dried herbs. Push a cinnamon stick into a caddy of black tea for a deliciously subtle cinnamon-flavoured tea, or add a whole vanilla pod to a tin of green Japanese Sencha for a slightly sweet, gently aromatic tea. Add dried mint leaves to green or black tea for a refreshing and soothing flavoured tea.

When creating own blends in large quantities, it is important to select teas with similar leaf sizes or the mixture will separate out in the packet or tin and give an uneven brew. So choose a Ceylon Orange Pekoe and a Kenyan Orange Pekoe to mix together; select a Broken Orange Pekoe Assam to blend with a Broken Orange Pekoe Ceylon; or mix an orthodox FOP or OP Darjeeling with an orthodox FOP or OP Nilgiri. If playing with flavours each time you brew, the size of leaf is not so crucial and you can simply try adding a pinch of Earl Grey to a favourite Ceylon, or a few leaves of Lapsang Souchong to Assam to give a touch of smokiness. Once blended, store the blend in an air-tight container in a dark, cool place, away from other smells. Flavoured teas can easily taint teas stored nearby so do make sure that packets and tins are really tightly sealed.

The trading of tea has changed radically over the past fifty years. At one time, London was the centre of the tea trade, with vast quantities arriving by ship from China and tea being offered at the London auctions to international buyers. England's earliest recorded auction of tea took place in London on 11 March 1679 and by the mid-18th century quarterly auctions of China teas were being held. In 1706, the auctions took place at Lord Craven's House in Leadenhall Street in the City of London, which became known as East India House. The tea was sold 'by the candle', whereby a candle, marked out into inches, was lit as bidding began and when one inch had burned away the hammer was brought down on a particular lot. In 1834, the auctions moved premises to the newly-built Commercial Salesrooms in nearby Mincing Lane and then in 1937 moved again to Plantation House, just down the road. In 1971, the auctions relocated to

East India House, 1802

Sir John Lyon House in Upper Thames Street and again in 1990 to the London Chamber of Commerce. Because of the changing nature of the tea trade and the setting up of auction centres in the producing countries, the London auctions closed in 1998.

Meanwhile, the producing countries had set up their own auctions where locally grown teas were offered to local and international buyers. In 1861, India held its first tea auctions in Calcutta. India now has auction centres in Calcutta, Guwahati (1970), Siliguri, Cochin (1948), Coonoor (1963) and Coimbatore (1980); Sri Lanka's centre was established in Colombo in 1883; the Chittagong auctions opened in 1949 to sell Bangladeshi tea; Kenya's Nairobi auctions began in 1956 and moved to Mombasa in 1969 (the Mombasa auctions sell teas from Uganda, Rwanda, Burundi and Tanzania); Limbe in Malawi opened in 1970; and Jakarta's Indonesian tea auctions first traded in 1972. Some teas from those countries, as well as teas from countries where there are no auctions, are traded by private treaties drawn up between producers and brokers.

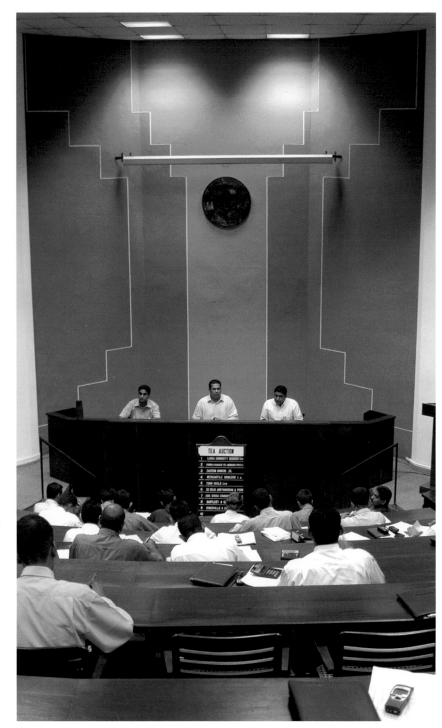

A typical auction scene ~ bidders gather to buy teas from different brokers in Colombo, Sri Lanka.

Before an auction is held, samples of tea are sent out by the producing estates and gardens to potential customers who taste them and assess which, if any, they wish to buy. Bids are then made at the auction in the normal way and the purchased lots are transported to the purchaser's warehouse.

The year 1982 saw the start of offshore auctions, whereby container-loads of tea are sold while still at sea. Samples will have been sent out in the usual way before potential buyers decide if they want to purchase the container-load. Offshore auctions have helped solve the problem in landed auctions of long delays in transferring money from the purchaser to the broker.

Since the London auctions closed, there have also been experiments in selling tea by electronic auction via the internet but this has been slow to take off and, without the support of the major world buyers, new websites have struggled to survive. In 2004, the Tea Board of India became the latest to try this method of trading tea.

When tea was first traded to Europe and America, the loose leaf was packed into tea chests. Today, bulk teas are packed into paper sacks (chests are still used for the more fragile large-leaf teas), loaded onto pallets, shrinkwrapped, placed inside containers, loaded onto container ships and dispatched to consuming countries all around the world. On arrival, the tea is unloaded and sent by truck to suitable warehousing facilities.

Most large tea blenders and packers buy vast quantities of tea from brokers and through auctions across the globe. They then blend the tea (see page 52) and pack it as teabags or loose packet tea, or they use it as a base for flavoured teas. Some tea companies have a close relationship with, or financial interests in, particular plantations and so buy direct from those estates. Smaller traders usually buy smaller quantities of tea from brokers and wholesalers and then pack them into smaller quantities ready for sale to the consumer.

Instead of only selling their tea in bulk through auction centres, some plantations now sell what is known as 'value added tea' direct from the estates to their customers – who may include supermarket chains or agents working in the different consuming countries. 'Value added teas' are teas that have been packed into teabags or packets and caddies at the factory rather than in bulk. The selection of teas offered generally includes a blended tea typical of the region, and a range of flavoured teas. The thinking behind this new approach is that it is worth investing in the necessary bagging and packaging machinery in order to take control of the way in which the local tea reaches the consumer. It also allows the individual producers to increase their profits. Furthermore, some producers of high-quality teas are now selling smaller quantities of their teas (two or three chests at a time) direct to smaller companies instead of putting all their tea into the auctions.

Tea Packaging

Over the centuries, the packaging of tea has also undergone major changes. Until the days of the Ming Dynasty (AD 1368–1644), China's compressed teas travelled well wrapped in bamboo, dried grasses or banana leaves and the tablets, tea balls and slabs retained their shape, quality and flavour. But the new fashion for loose-leaf tea that emerged during the Ming period meant that new packaging methods were required. Open bamboo baskets were useless, and heavy earthenware jars and lacquered boxes were too cumbersome to be practical. And so the tea chest was invented. Cheaper types of tea were packed into bamboo crates lined with wax paper, rice paper and bamboo paper, while more expensive, delicate teas were packed into decorative lacquer chests. Now the Chinese merchants could send their teas on the 18-month journey across the high seas to Europe without worrying constantly for the safety and quality of the product. Chests were gradually improved to create a truly air-tight container but the change from various papers to a lead lining was later recognized as a health hazard and aluminium or tin foil was used instead.

Ceylon, 1905

Today, tea chests are only used for expensive large-leafed teas which are easily crushed and need considerable protection during shipping. Chests are often made from the timber of shade trees which grow amongst the tea plants on the plantations. These shade trees protect the bushes from the glare of intensive sunlight and

The Tealover's Companion

need felling and replacing from time to time. This recycling of the wood helps to make the tea an environmentally ethical commodity. Some producers now use foil-lined boxes or cartons instead of wooden chests for their more fragile large-leaf teas and these vary in size and shape. For smaller-leafed varieties, chests and cartons have generally been replaced by paper sacks which are made from several layers of tough paper and aluminium foil, strong and thick enough to keep flavour in and humidity and odours out. There is no standard size for paper sacks and those in common usage can carry between 20 and 50 kilos of tea. For transportation, filled sacks are loaded onto pallets and wrapped tightly with several layers of shrinkwrap plastic.

In the retailing of tea, packaging has also changed dramatically over the centuries. In Europe, early consumers bought small quantities of tea in a 'screw' of paper. Merchants would sell 'straights' or blended teas – often specially made to individual clients' requirements. In the 19th century, with the market expanding and competition between merchants increasing rapidly, the idea of packaging loose tea in branded packets and boxes took off. For the first time, individual companies offered guaranteed exact weights and attracted customers by drawing on oriental images for the design of their caddies and packets.

Today, teas are available in a wide variety of caddies, tins and boxes, cardboard packages, decorative wooden caskets, foil-lined pouches, vacuum-packed tubs and porcelain jars, the most important feature being air-tight lids that shut out the air.

Storing Tea

The enemies of tea are humidity, air and light and it is extremely important that tea is carefully stored from the moment it leaves the drying machines in the factory to its arrival in the caddy or tin at home. Manufacturers must ensure that made tea is immediately transferred from drying and blending machines to sealed paper sacks or chests. The wholesaler must ensure that sacks and chests are kept closed and in cool, dry storage in the warehouse. Similarly, the retailer needs a clean, dry, cool storage space for spare stock, and air-tight storage tins or caddies on shop shelves from which to sell to customers. Ready-packed tins and packages of tea must be tightly sealed (and preferably re-sealable) so that once the customer has taken the tea home, it is easy to keep the tea fresh and air-tight.

At home it is always best to transfer both loose tea and teabags from a cardboard or paper packet or tub into an air-tight container of some sort.

Tins and caddies with really tight-fitting lids are best as they will keep out other smells and humidity. Air-tight glass jars on open shelves are not ideal for the storage of tea as light can damage the leaves and reduce the quality. If, however, the jars are stored in a dark cupboard, the tea will keep well. Tea should not be kept in the refrigerator as there is always a chance that water or water vapour will get into the packet. The only exception to this rule is Japanese Matcha, the powdered green tea used in the Japanese Tea Ceremony (see page 74). This tea does not keep well and small amounts are sold in vacuum-sealed containers which, in Japan, are usually kept in the refrigerator.

Be extra careful with flavoured teas. The added flavourings can be very powerful and easily taint other teas nearby. Similarly, take care when measuring tea from caddy or packet to teapot. Make sure that the spoon or scoop used is absolutely dry. If there is even a drop of moisture on the spoon, the humidity introduced to the interior of the packet or caddy will have a damaging effect on the quality and flavour.

Choosing What to Buy

With the increasingly wide variety of teas available today, it is sometimes difficult to decide what to buy. Ultimately, only by trying different types of tea will an individual tea-drinker be able to decide what he or she likes best for particular occasions. Wherever possible, buy small quantities of a tea to sample before buying larger quantities. Go to a retail store that can offer guidance and advice. Ask lots of questions about the tea itself, the best way to brew, how to store, whether the tea drinks well with milk, etc, and be aware of grading terms used on retailers' packets and tins. If you are not sure what they mean, ask more questions. A good retailer will be happy to discuss the different teas with you. Be aware also that the nature of the water in a particular region or country will make a difference to your experience of any one tea.

Loose Tea or Teabags?

The first important decision to be made when choosing a tea is whether to buy teabags or loose-leaf. Many people prefer teabags because they are easier to handle, the quantity of tea is already measured out, they do not present the problem of how to dispose of the wet leaves, they allow for the easy removal of the bag from the brew once the correct strength has been achieved and are generally convenient and quick to use. Some teabags are extremely disappointing because of the small amount and poor quality of the leaf inside the bag. However, there are companies that do offer very good teabags containing quality leaf. The latest trend is for bags made of nylon gauze (often referred to as 'crystal') or muslin. As well as being extremely sophisticated and stylish, these bags usually contain larger grades of leaf and allow the tea enough room to swell up and release its flavour and colour more successfully into the water.

Elegant crystal bags allow the tea to release the maximum amount of flavour.

Most true tea connoisseurs intensely dislike the idea of teabags and prefer always to choose a loose leaf. The advantages, as they see it, are that a much wider selection of loose-leaf teas is available from around the world, the brewer can decide what quantity and quality of tea to use, loose tea almost always gives a better, more subtle and fuller-flavoured brew than teabags and, for the connoisseur, the ritual of measuring out the leaves into the pot is an important part of the tea-brewing ceremony.

The case for teabags or loose tea:

ADVANTAGES OF TEABAGS

- easy to brew just one cup;
- quick and convenient;
- easy to separate tea from liquor once the brew has reached the correct strength;
- no untidy wet leaves to dispose of;
- useful for brewing large quantities of tea for special events, etc.

DISADVANTAGES OF TEABAGS

- do not offer the wide selection of world teas that are available as loose tea;
- contain small particles of tea that brew quickly but often lack subtlety of flavour;
- often do not allow the tea enough room to brew properly;
- the paper of the teabag stops the full flavour of the tea infusing out into the water;
- teabags lose their flavour and quality more quickly than loose-leaf tea;
- only small-leafed teas can be put into teabags.

ADVANTAGES OF LOOSE-LEAF TEA

- the consumer has an endless choice of world teas;
- the decision of how much tea to use is left to the consumer;
- the measuring of the leaf is a very important part of the traditional tea-brewing ceremony;
- the consumer can assess the quality of a tea from the appearance and aroma of the wet leaves as well as from the taste of the liquor.

DISADVANTAGES OF LOOSE-LEAF TEA

- if leaf tea is allowed to brew for too long the liquor will become bitter and harsh; it is preferable to separate the leaves from the water at the end of the correct brewing time by lifting out the infuser basket or by straining the tea liquor from the brewing pot into a second, clean, warm pot;
- perfect brewing needs careful measuring of the leaf and timing of the brew – actually not a disadvantage at all, but simply a vital element in the performance of brewing.

Perfect Brewing

Water for Tea

The type of water used for brewing plays an enormously important role in the final flavour, clarity and colour of the liquor. While a tea brewed in one particular water may taste dull and flat, the same tea brewed in water from a different location can be wonderfully brisk and bright. All the ingredients of an individual water play their part in the brewing process – the natural minerals, the added chemicals such as chlorine and fluoride, the amount of oxygen, etc.

To remove unwanted solubles, mains water needs to be passed through some kind of filtration system. Some filtration systems add various salts and minerals to the water and these can create different problems. The most effective types work according to a process known as 'Reverse Osmosis', whereby the water is passed through a membrane which forces unwanted chemicals and other deposits out of the water molecules to leave water that is approximately 99.4% pure.

Lu Yu (see page 7) recommended spring water as the best for tea because of its purity, freshness and high oxygen content. The poorest water for tea is water that has stood for any length of time and has therefore become lifeless and flat.

Hard water which contains a high level of calcium is poor for most types of tea, deadening the flavour and causing a scum to form on the surface of the tea in the cup, as calcium carbonate reacts with oxygen to become calcium bicarbonate. The addition of acid to the tea helps to eliminate the bicarbonate ions, and so adding a drop or two of lemon juice prevents scum from being formed. Adding sugar to the tea also reduces the development of scum but most teas are better without sugar and so this is not recommended.

If soft water and permanently hard water (that contains calcium sulphate) are used for tea, the liquor is usually bright and clear and the flavour brisk and lively. If bottled water is used, a pH of 7 is ideal. But choose carefully since many types of bottled water contain salts and other minerals which can spoil the flavour of the tea in the same way as can some tap water.

THE TEAPOT

The teapots used in the West today developed from the little round-bodied teapots that were imported from China to Europe and North America on the same ships that brought the tea. Whereas coffee pots have always been tall and usually straight-sided, teapots have retained their low, squat shape. The early imported pots were small because that is how the Chinese made and used their pots (and indeed still use them today), but as the cost of tea in Europe fell during the 18th and 19th centuries and tea became more of an everyday beverage, teapots grew in size.

The best teapots are those made in glazed stoneware, pottery, china, porcelain, and glass. Silver teawares have been popular since the late 17th century but silver does not necessarily make the best brewing vessel. Silver can hold the flavour of the last tea brewed in it and so needs very careful washing and rinsing after use.

Teapots that are glazed inside can be washed in a dishwasher or by hand using normal detergents. However, to be sure that the flavour of brewed tea is not tainted with residues of soap, always rinse the teapot very carefully. To restore a tea's flavour and aroma to a pot, spoon in a scoop of dry tea leaves, place the lid on the pot and leave to stand until the next time it is used, then empty out the dry leaves before the pot is re-used.

To remove tea stains from the inside and spout of a teapot, measure in two large spoonfuls of bicarbonate of soda, fill the pot with boiling water and leave to soak overnight. Rinse thoroughly and dry. Commercial cleaning products, such as Buster TSR (Tea and Coffee Stain Remover) are very effective but be sure to rinse the pot well before re-using.

YIXING TEAPOTS

Yixing is famous for its many coloured clays and for the teapots made from them. Since the 1500s, potters in this Chinese lake-side town have been fashioning the most exquisite unglazed teapots in the form of houses, lotus flowers, pumpkins, Buddhist priests, boxes, bundles of bamboo, dragons, fruit, vegetables, human figures and buildings. Yixing pots are said to be the best brewing vessels for oolong teas and because the interior of the pot is unglazed, each pot must only be used for one tea. Over time, the pot absorbs the flavour of the tea and builds up a patina that enhances future brews. For this reason, a Yixing pot should never be washed with soaps and detergents but should simply be rinsed and allowed to dry.

INFUSER AND PLUNGER TEAPOTS

The flavour of tea can become very unpleasant if the leaves stand for too long in the hot water, so many different pots are now available that contain their own purpose-designed infuser basket that can be lifted out, or that have a plunger (rather like the plunger in a cafetière) that allows the separation of the tea from the liquor once the tea has brewed.

An infuser teapot (left) and a plunger teapot (right)

When choosing a pot with an inbuilt infuser, make sure that the infuser basket or bag is large enough to allow the leaves to move around, swell up and release their colour and flavour into the water, and check that

the design allows the lid to sit neatly on the top of the pot both when the infuser is in the pot and after it has been lifted out. If choosing a plunger pot, make sure that the plunger really does separate the leaves from the water. As long as any of the leaves are in contact with the water, the tea will go on brewing.

INFUSERS

Also available today is a range of plastic, metal, cloth and paper infusers that allow the easy separation of the leaf from the water. Aluminium is not good as a material for these infusers as it taints the flavour of the tea, but chrome, porcelain, nylon, plastic, unbleached paper are all excellent – as long as they are large enough to allow the tea to brew properly. They should be designed so that they fit down into the bottom of the teapot, are easy to leave in the pot and easy to lift out once the tea has brewed.

Infuser mugs are also available. These act like a mini teapot and are a useful alternative in the workplace or kitchen.

THE GUYWAN

The *Guywan* (mandarin Chinese for 'covered cup'; in Cantonese, *Cha Chung* or *Zh*) is one of China's traditional brewing vessels. It consists of a deep bowl that has no handle, a lid and a saucer. The loose tea leaves are measured into the guywan, water is added and, with the lid in place, the leaves are allowed to brew. The liquor is then drunk from the cup while the lid is carefully angled to hold the leaves back inside the cup.

JAPANESE TEA BOWLS

The large, rather rough, handmade pottery bowls used for whisked tea during the Japanese Tea Ceremony have been made in the same way since the Japanese started drinking tea almost 1,200 years ago. They are thought to have developed from Korean rice bowls and, since most potters in Japan at that time came from Korea, it was this style that was adapted for tea. The bowls must be of a certain thickness; if they are too thin they will be too hot to hold and may allow the tea to cool too rapidly. Conversely, bowls that are too thick will not become sufficiently hot.

TEA HOTPLATES

Several companies now offer glass or metal hotplates on which to keep brewed tea warm. These should never be *too* hot and the little candle lights designed for use in them are ideal. Be sure never to stand a pot of tea on one of these special burners if the leaves are still in the pot.

TEA COSIES

Tea cosies are useful for keeping a pot of tea warm but should never be used if the tea leaves are still in the pot, as the tea will become bitter and unpleasant.

CADDY SPOONS AND SCOOPS

The ideal scoop or measure for spooning tea from caddy or packet to pot holds approximately 2.5 grams. The perfect measure for most teas is 2.5–3 grams of tea to 190–200ml (6½–7fl oz) of water. This varies according to the type of tea used and to personal taste.

Brewing Methods

The method of brewing tea differs according to the individual tea and to the traditional tea culture of the country in question.

BREWING BLACK TEA IN A TEAPOT

1   Select a teapot of the correct size for the number of cups required.
2   Fill a kettle or pan with freshly drawn cold water and bring to the boil.
3   When the water is almost boiling, pour a little into the teapot, swill it around and then pour the water away.
4   Measure the loose tea or count the teabags (allowing one bag per cup to be brewed) into the teapot and when the water in the kettle is just coming to a rolling boil, pour the water onto the leaves or bags. Whenever possible, place the leaves inside an infuser that can then be lifted out of the liquid once the tea has brewed. Allow 2.5–3 grams of tea per 190–200ml cup.
5   Put the lid on the pot and set a timer to the correct number of minutes for the tea being brewed. For small-leafed teas, allow 2–3 minutes, for large-leafed teas, allow 3–5 minutes, depending on personal taste.
6   After the correct number of minutes, lift the infuser containing the leaves out of the pot and discard. If not using an infuser, immediately strain all the tea into cups or into another heated pot to keep warm. Discard the leaves, or if the tea is of a variety that will give a second and possibly a

third infusion, add more water and leave to brew for the required number of minutes.

7   Keep the pot warm on a special hotplate that is heated by a candle light or cover the pot with a cosy. Never keep a pot of tea hot in this way if the leaves are still in the pot – the tea will stew and taste extremely bitter and unpleasant.

BREWING GREEN TEA IN A TEAPOT

Follow the steps for brewing black tea but never pour boiling water onto green tea. Green leaves prefer a slightly cooler temperature so pour water from the kettle into an empty pot or jug and allow to cool to approximately 80–85°C (176–180°F) before pouring onto the tea.

Brewing times for green teas vary. Most Chinese greens need 3–4 minutes, while Japanese teas brew very quickly and need to be separated from the water after 1–2 minutes or less. Some of Japan's most expensive green teas need water at 50–60°C (122–140°F).

BREWING WHITE TEA

The brewing time for different white teas varies. Some need 4–6 minutes while others may need up to 10 minutes. Chinese white teas generally need 5–6 minutes for the first steeping and slightly longer for subsequent steepings. Darjeeling whites need only 3–5 minutes.

Some white teas will yield more infusions than others. A good-quality Yin Zhen (Silver Needles) will give up to five or six infusions and each will have its own unique individual character. A Darjeeling white will give two or three infusions.

1   Bring freshly drawn cold water to the boil and allow it to cool to the same temperature as for oolong teas (so as not to scald the leaf). This is about 85–88°C (185–190°F).

2   Measure the leaves into a teapot, glass or guywan, allowing 3–4 grams of leaf to 7–8fl oz of water.

3   Pour on the water, cover and allow to brew for between 3 and 10 minutes, depending on the type of tea.

4   Strain and add more water for further infusions.

The 'gongfu' brewing method allows the preparation of several short infusions from one measure of leaves, each infusion having its own distinct character. It should be carried out using a small Yixing earthenware teapot. You also need tall, straight-sided smelling cups, small, shallow drinking bowls and a waterproof tray on which to place all the equipment (waterproof because the various vessels are heated while standing on the tray by having hot water poured over them). With a traditional set of brewing equipment, the tray has its own draining devise to carry away the water.

1 Start by pouring hot water into the little teapot to warm it and then pour that water away.

2 For brewing black, oolong and puerh teas by this method rinse the leaves and prepare them for the brewing process. Measure the tea leaves into the pot (2.5–3gms per 190–200ml cup) and pour in enough hot or boiling water to half fill it. Place the lid on the pot and drain off all the liquid. For green tea, leave out this rinsing stage of the brewing ceremony.

3 Warm the little drinking bowls by pouring hot water into them and then draining the water out.

4 Add more water to the teapot, put the lid on the pot and pour more water over the pot. For oolong tea allow about 1 minute, for green tea allow 2–3 minutes and for black tea allow 3 minutes.

5 Immediately strain the tea liquor into a second teapot or bowl before pouring it into the tall, straight-sided smelling cups.

6 Place a small drinking bowl upside down on top of the smelling cup and invert it carefully so that the tea flows into the drinking bowl. The aroma of the tea can then be enjoyed in the smelling cup and the tea may be sipped from the little bowl.

7 Add more water to the leaves in the pot for a second and third infusion.

1   Start by rinsing the leaves. To do this, measure the tea into the guywan and
    pour on boiling or hot water. Using the lid to hold the leaves back, tip
    away all the water. Lift off the lid and inhale the wonderful aroma of the
    leaves.

2   Add more water to the cup, allowing it to run down the inside of the ves-
    sel rather than pouring it directly onto the leaves. This makes the leaves
    swirl in the cup and helps them to brew correctly.

3   Cover the guywan with its lid and allow the leaves to brew for the correct
    number of minutes: 1 for oolong, 2–3 for green and 3–4 for black.

4   To drink the tea, lift the three pieces of the guywan together and place
    comfortably in the palm of the right hand, using the thumb to hold the
    cup steady. With the first and second fingers and thumb of the left hand,
    lift the lid and tilt it so that it restrains the leaves inside the cup as the cup
    is tipped for drinking. The position of the thumb against the nose during
    sipping hinders the drinker from tilting the cup too far. This is good be-
    cause the guywan should not be completely emptied but should have more
    water added while some of the infusion is still in the cup.

5   Go on adding fresh hot water as many times as the tea leaves allow.

Perfect Brewing

BREWING JAPANESE GREEN TEA

For a good-quality Sencha, choose a small teapot and small drinking bowls.

1   Bring freshly drawn water to the boil and pour some into the pot and bowls to warm them. Leave for 30–40 seconds and then pour the water away.

2   Measure approximately 2 teaspoons of tea into the pot and pour on approximately 200ml (7fl oz) of hot water at 80°C (176°F).

3   Allow to steep for 2 minutes then pour into the warmed bowls, pouring a little into each and then topping up with more tea from the pot so that each cup gets an even distribution of flavour.

4   Add more hot water to the leaves and allow to steep for a further 3 minutes to give a second, slightly stronger infusion.

With lower-quality Sencha, use water at approximately 90°C (194°F) and allow the tea to steep for only 30–60 seconds. For Bancha, Houjicha and Genmaicha, use a larger pot, boiling water and a short infusing time of not more than 30 seconds. For Gyokuro, use water at 60°C (140°F) and steep for 2–3 minutes. Add more water and steep the second infusion for 1–1½ minutes.

PREPARING TEA FOR THE JAPANESE TEA CEREMONY

The tea used for the traditional Japanese Tea Ceremony is a fine green-powdered tea called Matcha (see page 128). To prepare Matcha, you need a traditional tea bowl, a tea scoop (called a *chashaku*) and a bamboo whisk (called a *chasen*). If you don't have these use a teaspoon and a metal whisk.

1   Bring some water to the boil and then allow to cool.

2   Pour some hot water into the bowl and place the whisk in the water to warm it. After a few minutes, pour away the water. Scoop one and a half *chashaku* measures or two-thirds of a teaspoon of Matcha into the bowl.

3   Pour on a quarter of a bowl of the cooled water – the perfect temperature is 80°C (176°F) – and whisk briskly until little bubbles form on the surface of the tea.

The Directory

The following pages are a guide to 80 World Teas. For each one, the tea is shown as a dry leaf, a wet leaf, and an infusion (unless otherwise marked).

E.g.

Tea-growing areas on this and subsequent maps are denoted in green.

China

In the early days of cultivation in China, small plantations were often tended by Buddhist monks on land around their mountain-top temples and monasteries and, since the Chinese have always believed that 'famous teas come from high mountains', these plantations often produced some of the finest and best known teas.

In the past, strict rules governed the manual gathering of the new leaf buds and leaves. The timing of the harvest was crucial and all teas were gathered before the spring rains encouraged fast growth of the new shoots. The pickers were always young girls who would go out into the plantations in small groups very early in the morning and gather the young tender leaves into wicker baskets. It was vital that these pickers had immaculately clean fingernails and that they never ate garlic, onions, or other strongly flavoured foods that could change the smell of their skin and contaminate the teas they picked. Once the teas had been processed and packed, Chinese merchants sold more than 8,000 different types of tea, which were classified by the different methods of manufacture, by region and by leaf grade.

Today, tea is grown and produced in sixteen different regions – Anhui, Fujian, Guangdong, Guangxi Zhuang, Guizhou, Hainan, Henan, Hubei, Hunan, Jiangsu, Jiangxi, Shaanxi, Shandong, Sichuan, Yunnan and Zhejiang. The names by which the different teas are sold can be confusing. Names may give information about the garden where the tea grew, the time of year when the leaves were picked, the village or province, the method of manufacture used, any additional flavourings blended with the leaves, and perhaps also a legendary name. Further confusions arise because the Chinese refer to what we call 'black' tea as 'red' and because there are different dialectical languages and spellings used in the different regions. Names may be in Fukienese, which is spoken in Fujian; Cantonese, which is spoken in Canton; or English, if a particular type of tea has been marketed by that name since trade with Europe began. For example, Meigui Hongcha in Pinyin is Mui Kwai Hung Cha in Cantonese but the tea is usually marketed as Rose Pouchong or Rose Black. And Pinyin Tie Guanyin becomes Tit Koon Tam in Cantonese, Ti Kwan Yin for the international market, and translates as Tea of the Iron Goddess of Mercy. As well as its individual name, each tea is also given a grade number that indicates to customers that the tea is of a given standard. And some retailers and suppliers also add a 'chop' mark to their packaging that gives further information about the type of bush the tea came from, the season it was harvested and the finishing style used.

Many of China's finest teas are still made by hand and the skills needed for their manufacture are passed down from one generation to another. Today, more and more people around the world are beginning to appreciate the superb quality and fascinating histories of the vast array of white, yellow, green, black, oolong, puerh, compressed and scented teas that are now more widely available.

Because of restrictions of space, it has only been possible to include a small selection of teas from China. There are many more fascinating varieties available today.

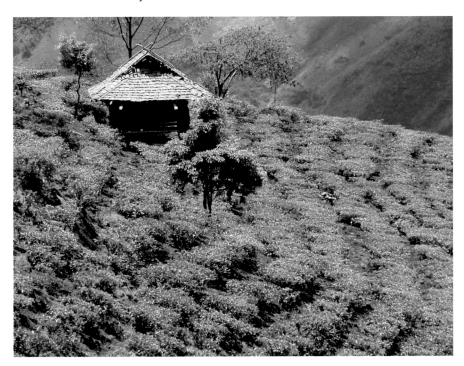

China

Baihao Yinzhen (Yinfeng, Silver Needle White Fur)

Produced in Fujian province, this exquisite tea is made only from new buds that are picked before they start to open. 'Baihao' (pek-ho) refers to the tiny white hairs on the underside of each tightly curled leaf bud and which give the tea its beautiful silvery velvet appearance. Yinzhen is picked for only a few days each spring and is sometimes also referred to as Silvery Tip Pekoe or Fujian White.

Character
The neatly pointed silver buds stand upwards in the water to give a pale yellow liquor that is smooth, sweet and extremely elegant.

Brewing Tips
Brew 5g in 200ml (7fl oz) water at 76°C (170°F) for 2 minutes. Strain and add more water to the leaves for a second infusion. Alternatively, for just one infusion, brew for 12–15 minutes.

Bai Mudan (Pai Mutan, White Peony)

A Fujian white tea, this is made from tightly curled buds picked with two or three tender young leaves. When they have been steamed and dried they have the appearance of little bunches of silver white blossoms (the silver leaf bud) set amongst lightly curled green and pale brown leaves.

Character
The leaves are a combination of tips, broken leaf and larger unbroken leaf in colours that range from white to dark green and ochre. The clear, very pale yellow infusion has a sweet muscatel aroma and a velvet smooth, sweet and mild flavour with a hint of nuttiness.

Brewing Tips
This can be brewed either as a green tea, an oolong or even as a black tea, depending on the temperature of the water you choose and the length of time the leaves are steeped. Infuse 4–5g in 200ml (7fl oz) water at 93°C (200°F) for 1½–2 minutes. Strain and add more water for a second infusion. Alternatively, for one infusion, steep for 6–7 minutes.

China

Huangshan Maofeng (Yellow Mountain Hair Peak)

The legend of this tea tells how a beautiful young tea picker was in love with a young man from the same village but the local tyrant kidnapped her to make her his concubine. She managed to escape but discovered that the tyrant had killed her lover and she found his body hidden deep in the mountains. She wept so much over the body that her tears became like rain and turned him into a tea bush. Grown on the mist-covered Huang Mountain in Anhui province, the tea bushes grow amongst wild peach trees.

Character
This small-leafed yellow tea is made from one leaf and one silvery bud and the dry leaf has a faintly herbal note. As it brews, it gives a very pale yellow liquor that has a rich peachy aroma and a uniquely rich, fruity, slightly nutty flavour.

Brewing Tips
Brew 5g in 200ml (7fl oz) water at 82°C (180°F) and infuse for 2 minutes. Strain and add more water for two further infusions.

This very attractive 'yellow bud' tea from Anhui province has large, lovingly hand-crafted leaves and downy silver buds.

Character
The tea is notable for the deeply floral character of its infusion. It is rich, full and smooth.

Brewing Tips
Brew 2–4g in 200ml (7fl oz) water at 70°C (160°F) for 1–2 minutes. Strain and add more water for three to four further infusions.

China

Jun Shan Yin Zhen (Jun Mountains Silver Needle)

Silver Needle consists of only the very young, silvery, down-covered buds that are harvested in early spring. The white bushes of northern Fujian province were domesticated from wild tea trees and exhibit silvery down-covered leaves that have been prized for their medicinal properties for more than 1,000 years.

Character
The buds stand upright when brewing and give a pale yellow infusion with a buttery texture and a mild aroma.

Brewing Tips
Brew 5g in 225ml (8fl oz) water at 76°C (170°F) for 2 minutes. Strain and add more water to the leaves for a second and third infusion.

Biluochun (Pi Lo Chun, Green Snail Spring)

This famous tea comes from two mountains in Jiangsu province known as East and West Dongting. The bushes grow in very humid conditions surrounded by fruit trees and so absorb the aroma of the blossoms in early spring when the tender leaves of the tea bush are just beginning to form. One new bud and one leaf are plucked and processed by hand into neat little spirals that look like tiny snails.

Character

The curled leaves are covered in fine white hairs and untwist to give a clear, green to pale golden-yellow liquor that has a wonderfully delicate and fragrant aroma and a clean aromatic flavour.

Brewing Tips

Brew 5g in 225ml (8fl oz) water at 76°C (170°F) for 2 minutes. Strain and add more water to the leaves for a second and third infusion.

China

Hai Bei Tu Zhu (Treasure of the Sea)

Tea and art combine to make this tea seashell. Green leaves are carefully formed by hand into the shape of a clam shell. Hidden inside is a row of tiny plum blossom buds and a centre of chrysanthemum flower. The tea is infused with jasmine.

Character
During brewing, the shell gradually opens and reveals the hidden blossoms inside. The liquor is clear and pale and has the heady perfume and flavour of jasmine blossoms.

Brewing Tips
Brew one piece in 170ml (6fl oz) water at 82°C (180°F) for 2 minutes. Add more water as required for two further infusions.

Jade Rings

These rings are made in Guanshan by meticulously hand-rolling silvery-white, green tea shoots into small rings.

Character
When infused, the little rings open up to create a magnificent cup of tea. The flavour from these early spring buds is subtle, sweet and classic.

Brewing Tips
Infuse 5g in 225ml (8fl oz) water at 82°C (180°F) for 1–2 minutes.

Jin Shang Tian Hua (Brocade of Flowers)

This beautiful 'display' flower of green tea is made by threading green leaves together with three small chrysanthemums hidden in the centre.

Character
As the tea opens in hot water, the flowers float upwards and weave a gentle meandering dance in the pale golden liquor.

Brewing Tips
Using a glass to brew so that you can enjoy the visual beauty of the tea, infuse one flower in 170ml (6fl oz) water at 82°C (180°F) for 2 minutes. Add more water as required for a second and third infusion.

China

Longjing (Lung Ching, Dragon Well)

This tea is named after the village where it grows in Zhejiang province. The best grade is made from one new bud and one new leaf; it is not rolled or shaped but left in its natural, neatly pointed form. The next grade, Queshe Longjing (Sparrow's Tongue), is made with a bud and two new leaves which open during brewing to look like a bird's beak and tongue. The teas are famous for their beautiful green colour, elegant shape, smooth flavour and fine aroma.

Character
The buds point upwards while brewing and release a clear, light yellowy-green colour. The clean well-balanced aroma suggests freshly cut grass and toasted chestnuts. The flavour is mellow with a bittersweet-savoury finish.

Brewing Tips
Brew 3g in 200ml (7fl oz) water at 82°C (180°F) for 2–3 minutes. Strain and add more water for two further infusions.

Green leaves are bundled together, tied with a fine thread and then rolled back on themselves to form a ball the size of a lychee fruit.

Character
During brewing, the leaves swell and become a green blossom that gives a clear green infusion with citrus notes.

Brewing Tips
Brew one flower in 170ml (6fl oz) water at 88°C (190°F) for 3 minutes. Add more water for three further infusions.

This green tea rosette from Hubei is made in the early spring by tying bundles of long tender leaves and buds together with a silk thread and then folding them back on themselves. As the tea brews, the leaves open into a beautiful bloom.

Character
As the flower infuses, it releases a pale golden colour and gives a sweet aroma. The infusion is mild with pleasant grassy notes and a refreshing finish.

Brewing Tips
Brew one flower in 225ml (8fl oz) water at 82°C (180°F) for 3–4 minutes. Add more water for two further infusions.

China

Tianmu Qingding (Tianmu Green Summit, From the Very Top)

Mount Tianmu in Zheijiang province has two peaks, known as East and West Tianmu. The air around the mountain tops and in the valleys is misty, warm and humid and tea bushes that grow there yield a highly prized tea that is often also known as 'Cloud and Mist'. Mount Tianmu, whose name translates as 'Eyes Looking Heavenward', was mentioned in Lu Yu's *Classic of Tea* in AD 780. The leaves are often used for making jasmine and magnolia flavoured teas.

Character
The tight, dark green strips of leaf are made from little sets of one bud and two tender leaves that are covered with tiny hairs. They infuse to give a clear strong brew that has a slightly nutty fragrance and flavour.

Brewing Tips
Infuse 2.5g in 200ml (7fl oz) water at 84°C (185°F) for 2 minutes. Strain and add more water for several further infusions.

Young Hyson (Flourishing Spring, Lucky Dragon)

As its name indicates, this is made from young leaves gathered in the early spring before the first rains fall. The leaves are twisted into long, thin strips.

Character
The leaves yield a golden-yellow liquor that has a smooth robust flavour and a pungent aftertaste.

Brewing Tips
Infuse 2.5g in 200ml (7fl oz) water at 76°C (170°F) for 2 minutes.

Zhen Mei (Chun Mei, Chunmee, Precious Eyebrows)

It is the curved shape of the dried leaves that gives this tea its name. Made in Yunnan province, the manufacturing process demands great skill. Each leaf must be rolled at the correct temperature, for the correct amount of time, to achieve the desired curve.

Character
The gently curved dark jade leaves give a light amber liquor with a soft, smooth, slightly plummy flavour.

Brewing Tips
Brew 2.5g in 200ml (7fl oz) water at 82°C (180°F) for 3 minutes.

China

Zhu Mei Xue Lian (Snow Lotus)

To make this exquisite, extremely rare tea, green tea leaves are bundled carefully together and a flower is then tied to the leaves and hidden inside. The bundle is then shaped to resemble a lotus pod, before being steamed and dried.

Character
As the lotus pod absorbs water, it slowly uncurls to reveal the flower hidden in the centre. The infusion has a smoky, smooth flavour.

Brewing Tips
Brew one Snow Lotus in a glass of 225g (8fl oz) water at 82°C (180°F) for 3 minutes. Add more water as required for three further infusions.

Zu Cha (Pearl Gunpowder)

Most Gunpowder teas are made in Zhejiang province and get their name from the fact that the tightly rolled little 'pearls' of tea look like pellets of gunpowder. Pearl Gunpowder is sold in various sizes from very small 'Pinhead' to larger, more loosely rolled varieties. It was originally marketed in Europe as 'Green Pearl' tea.

Character
The little pellets gradually open in hot water to release their warm amber colour and to give a mellow, quite strong, slightly astringent flavour with a lasting aftertaste.

Brewing Tips
Brew 4–5g in 200ml (7fl oz) water at 87°C (190°F) for 2 minutes. Add more water for a second and third infusion.

Phoenix Supreme Oolong

Hand-picked from bushes that grow on the Wudong peak of Phoenix Mountain in Guangdong province, this tea is made in small batches by experienced tea masters. The leaves are gathered twice a year (in April–May and October–November), when they are half-open, and processed by the special Phoenix method of 'rattling' the leaves and partial oxidation that lasts for 8–10 hours.

Character
The greeny-brown leaves are tightly twisted fine strips. The light-golden clear liquor has a fragrant fruity aroma and a smooth, very refreshing flavour.

Brewing Tips
Brew 3–4g in 150ml (5fl oz) water at 85°C (185°F) for 1 minute 15 seconds. Strain and add more water for one further infusion.

China

Qing Xiang Dan Cong (Pure Fragrance Oolong)

All quality oolong teas develop a delicate, often fruity or floral aroma and flavour during processing and this tea has a particularly powerful fragrance.

Character
A medium oxidized oolong tea that yields an exhilarating aroma and complex, multilayered infusion with a unique pear element.

Brewing Tips
Brew 5g in 200ml (7fl oz) water at 87°C (180°F) for 1.5 minutes. Strain and add more water for three further infusions.

Ti Kuan Yin (Tieguanyin, Tea of the Iron Goddess of Mercy)

Probably the best known of Chinese oolongs, this aromatic and elegant tea comes from central Fujian province. Its legend tells how a tea grower in the area would walk past an iron statue of Kuan Yin, the Goddess of Mercy, on his way to work each day. The statue stood in a small temple that was rather dilapidated and, although he could not afford to actually repair the building, the tea grower started to take care of it, cleaning it and lighting incense. Then one night, in a dream, the goddess told him to look in a cave behind the temple for a treasure that was hidden there. When he looked the next day he found a single tea shoot which he nurtured and cultivated. He named the tea Ti Guanyin.

Character
The crinkly, slightly twisted leaves are a mixture of reddy-brown and dark green and as they brew, they unfurl to give lace-edged leaves that release a honey-coloured liquor, a sweet, floral aroma and an orchid-like, smooth, delicate flavour.

Brewing Tips
Brew 3.5g in 200ml (7fl oz) water at 95°C (200°F) for 1.5–2 minutes. Add more water for two or three further infusions.

Dragon Whiskers

From Anhui province, this tea is aptly named for its bundles of black leaves that are bound together in colourful silk threads. This is also available as a green tea.

Character
The dark twisted leaves and furry tips yield a golden infusion that has a robust aroma and a sweet nutty flavour with a long smooth finish.

Brewing Tips
Pull the end of the thread and unwind from around the leaves. Brew one piece in 225ml (8fl oz) water at 100°C (212°F) for 3 minutes. Add more water for two further infusions.

China

Hong Mudan (Black Sea Anemone)

This black, display tea is made in southern Anhui province on a remote mountain where virtually every family grows tea. The 'anemones' are made from quality, spring-picked leaves that are then tied into beautiful rosettes. The tea is meant to be enjoyed for its visual appeal as well as for its fragrance and flavour.

Character
As it brews, the rosette infurls to resemble a sea anemone. The fragrance and flavour are sweet and delicate.

Brewing Tips
Brew one rosette in a glass of 225ml (8fl oz) water at 85°C (185°F) for several minutes to allow the rosette to gradually bloom. Add more water as required and the rosette will continue to give colour and flavour without becoming bitter.

Qimen Hao Ya (Keemun Downy Bud)

This shiny black tea is named after the area where it is produced – Qimen in Anhui province – and is considered to be among the élite of Chinese teas. Keemuns come in different grades but all have a similar jet-black appearance and are often used as a quality, well-balanced base for flavoured teas.

Character
The tightly twisted, slender jet-black leaves give a rich coppery brew that has a sweet floral aroma and a satisfyingly rich, winey flavour.

Brewing Tips
Brew 2.5g in 200ml (7fl oz) water at 100°C (212°F) for 3 minutes. Add more water for a second and third infusion.

Qimen Mao Feng (Keemun Hair Peak)

Mao Feng translates as 'hairpoint', referring to the long, fine, tightly twisted strips of leaf that make up this highly prized tea. This is the highest grade and least processed of the traditional 'Burgundy' of teas.

Character
The leaves release a rich, dark brown liquor that has an orchid-like aroma and a complex, full-bodied flavour.

Brewing Tips
Brew 2.5g in 200ml (7fl oz) water at 100°C (212°F) for 2 minutes. Add more water for a second infusion.

China

Tanyang Golden Rim

Yunnan Gold

From the Fuding area of northern Fujian province, this tea is made from leaves gathered in the early spring. The name comes from the golden rim that can be seen around the surface of the amber infusion in the cup or bowl.

Character
The golden brown leaves show a good proportion of golden tip and yield a memorable, sophisticated smoothness with a hint of peach. The long finish has a satisfying sweetness that lingers on the tongue.

Brewing Tips
Brew 2.5g in 150ml (5fl oz) water at 95°C (200°F) for 2–5 minutes.

Yunnan province has been producing teas for more than 1,700 years. The black teas from this region are made from the leaves of the local broad-leafed variety of the tea bush and the tea displays big golden buds and uni-form-shaped leaves.

Character
The black leaves have a generous scat-tering of golden buds and brew to give a liquor that is a rich, dark reddish-black with a molasses-like sweetness and malty finish.

Brewing Tips
Brew 2.5g in 225ml (8fl oz) water at 100°C (212°F) for 4–5 minutes.

Zengshan Xiaozhong
(Lapsang Souchong, Smoked Tea)

Lapsang Souchong teas are a speciality of Fujian province. Souchong means 'sub-variety' and refers to the type of tea bush that grows in the Wuyi Mountains. The leaves are withered over pine or cypress wood fires and then pan-fried and rolled. Next they are pressed into wooden barrels, covered with a cloth and left to oxidize. Then the leaves are fried and rolled into tight strips. Finally, they are hung in baskets over smoking pine wood fires to dry.

Character
The intensely black leaves give a dark red liquor that has a distinctive smoky aroma and flavour.

Brewing Tips
Brew 2.5g in 200ml (7fl oz) water at 100°C (212°F) for 2–4 minutes. Strain and add more water to the leaves for a second and third infusion.

China

Tuo Cha

This compressed tea is like a very neat round bird's nest. It is made by pressing oxidized steamed Puerh leaves into cakes and then leaving the tea to age.

Character
This gives a rich, dark brew that has the typical earthy aroma and flavour of Puerh teas.

Brewing Tips
Break off 3–5g and steep in 200ml (7fl oz) water at 100°C (212°F) for 2–3 minutes.

Xiao Tuo Cha (Mini Tuo Cha, Small Bowl Tea)

This is made with a select grade of Puerh which is hand-harvested from 1,300-year-old trees on Jing Mai Mountain in Yunnan. Each mini bowl is individually wrapped.

Character
This tea gives a surprisingly rich and sweet infusion with a full body and smooth finish that is not generally found in most Mini Tuo Cha grades.

Brewing Tips
Like most Puerh teas, Mini Tuo Cha can be steeped several times. Steep one mini bowl in 225ml (8fl oz) water at 100°C (212°F) for 3–4 minutes.

wet leaf

Hubei Hong Zhuan Cha
(Hubei Black Brick Tea)

Puerh Bamboo Tea

This is a half-size version of the larger compressed tea bricks. Each side is decorated with a traditional design pressed into the tea.

Earthy leaves from remote areas of Yunnan province are compressed into discs and stored inside a segment of bamboo.

Character
When crushed and steeped, the compressed brick tea gives a rich, dark infusion with a strong aroma and flavour.

Character
The compressed Puerh yields a dark reddy-brown brew with a typical aged earthy aroma and flavour.

Brewing Tips
Crush and brew 2.5g in 200ml (7fl oz) water at 100°C (212°F) for 3 minutes. Strain and add more water for two further infusions.

Brewing Tips
Brew half a disc in 200ml (7fl oz) water at 100°C (212°F) for 2 minutes. Strain and add more water for two further infusions.

wet leaf

wet leaf

China

Loose-leaf Puerh (Ming Cha)

Jasmine Pearl

Loose-leaf Puerhs demonstrate clearly how large the leaves of the ancient Yunnan bushes are. They vary in colour from golden brown to rich black and all have the distinctive woody, elemental aroma of Puerhs.

Character
Large twisted leaves that yield a rich earthy flavour and aroma.

Brewing Tips
Infuse 2.5g in 200ml (7fl oz) water at 100°C (212°F) for 3 minutes. Strain and add more water for two further infusions.

Jasmine teas are produced in Fujian, Jiangsu, Anhui, Hubei, Zhejiang and Sichuan provinces according to tea-scenting techniques that date back more than 900 years. They come as loose-leaf teas and as different-sized spheres. This 'pearl' tea is made by tightly rolling fine, tender, green leaves and buds which are then infused with the essence of fresh jasmine blossoms. After scenting, the jasmine flowers are removed, leaving only the jasmine-scented tea pearls.

Character
The little pearls of tea open up during brewing to release their pale greeny-yellow colour in the water and to give a powerful heady aroma of jasmine flowers. The flavour is sweet, smooth, clean and beautifully perfumed.

Brewing
Use a glass or a glass teapot so you can enjoy the visual beauty of the little pearls opening and floating in the water. Brew 2g of jasmine pearls in 225ml (8fl oz) water at 87°C (190°F) for 3–4 minutes.

Jasmine teas are traditionally made by scenting green tea with fresh jasmine flowers. The flowers are picked during the day but stored until the evening when they open to release their heady perfume. The tea is heaped beside the flowerheads to allow absorption of the perfume. After several hours, when the heat produced by the tea begins to increase, the leaves are spread out and reheaped for further scenting. Alternatively, the tea is layered with jasmine flowers.

Character
Loose, lightly fermented pouchong leaves mixed with delicate dried jasmine petals infuse to give a pale amber liquor that has a powerfully perfumed aroma and flavour.

Brewing Tips
Brew 3.5g in 200ml (7fl oz) water at 87°C (190°F) for 2 minutes. Strain and add more water for two further infusions.

China

Lanhsiang (Lanxiang) Orchid Scented

Meigui Hongcha (Rose Congou, Rose Petal Black)

Most of China's flavoured and scented teas are made from green leaves, but some oolongs and blacks are also blended with flower fragrances. Orchid-scented teas are perfumed with flowers of the *Chloranthus Spicatus*.

'Congou' comes from the Chinese word Kungfu, which has to do with skill and dedicated learning. Congou teas all consist of carefully made, neat, unbroken black leaf. Rose Congou is blended with dried pink rose petals.

Character
Neat browny-black leaves give an amber liquor that has a sweetly perfumed aroma and an exotic and luxurious flavour.

Character
Neat black pieces of leaf and curled pink rose petals give a powerfully fragrant aroma and a warm coppery infusion that is smooth, mellow and gently flavoured with sweet roses.

Brewing Tips
Infuse 2.5g in 200ml (7fl oz) water at 87°C (200°F) for 1–2 minutes. Strain and add more water for one or two further infusions.

Brewing Tips
Brew 2.5g in 200ml (7fl oz) water at 100°C (212°F) for 3 minutes. Strain and add more water for one or two further infusions.

Georgia

RUSSIA

BLACK
SEA

● Kutaisi

Batumi
●

■ Tbilisi

Bolnisi ●

TURKEY   ARMENIA   AZERBAIJAN

Georgia grows tea in the fertile foothills of the snow-capped Caucasus Mountains that form the border between Georgia and Russia. Conditions here are ideal for tea cultivation – clean air, fertile soil, organic farming methods and plenty of rain and clear running water. Tea was first cultivated here in 1890 and because the tea produced was so good, under Russian control the area became the main source of tea for Soviet samovars. New technology was introduced, including mechanical harvesters and factory machines, and the long-term effect was to reduce the quality of Georgian tea. Since independence from Russia, however, Georgia and the rest of the world are discovering the country's fine and unusual 'hand-made' teas, for, although the outside world knew nothing of their activities, Georgian families have for decades been quietly making black tea by hand in their farmhouses. And now, with the help of British consultant Nigel Melican, these Georgian teas are finding their way onto the world market.

Since 2003, around 500 families from West Georgia have joined together to form the Tea Producer Farmers' Association – Caucasus Tea. Members must produce either 'hand-made' tea, made entirely by hand without the use of any machinery at all, or 'village-made tea', made using

small-scale, locally designed machinery that in many cases has been made by the village blacksmith. Older members who have been making tea all their lives are passing on their skills and knowledge to the younger generation. Each tea maker picks his or her own leaf and develops a unique, individual way of rolling, bruising, twisting, withering, oxidizing and drying the leaves. The teas are classified by and marketed under the name of the person who made it.

Natela's Tea GOPA

Natela Gujabidze has been making tea in her village of Nagobileui in Western Georgia all her life. She makes the tea entirely by hand and the fine long leaves are gently hand-rolled and then dried in the Georgian sunshine.

Character
The browny-black, twisted tangle of leaves is flecked with distinct golden tips. The infusion this gives is mid-amber in colour and has a deliciously sweet and mellow flavour with a hint of citrus and chestnut. After brewing, the leaves have the appearance of an oolong, with a rich mix of ruddy brown and dark green.

Brewing Tips
Brew 2.5g in 200ml (7fl oz) water at 100°C (212°F) for 5 minutes.

Ilia's Tea OP1

Ilia Basilashvili makes a 'village-made tea' using finely plucked leaf and a small home-made rolling table and rotary dryer.

Character
The very dark browny-black leaf is rather like a small version of a Yunnan tea in appearance. Some of the pieces of leaf are lightly curved, others straighter. It brews to give a bright, clear, dark amber infusion that has the aroma of honey and is sweet and smooth.

Brewing Tips
Brew 2.5g in 200ml (7fl oz) water at 100°C (212°F) for 5 minutes.

MILK IN TEA

In the early days of tea-drinking in Britain, milk was not a regular addition to the cup. The custom seems to have started at the end of the 17th century and perhaps developed because milk and cream were found to soften the slightly bitter taste of tea. The Dutch drank what they called 'melk-thee', perhaps as a result of their contact with the Manchu Dynasty that was ruling China at the time when contact between the two countries began. A Dutch traveller, Jean Nieuhoff, wrote of his experience of tea with milk at a banquet given by the Chinese emperor for a visiting Dutch delegation in 1655. 'At the beginning of dinner,' he wrote, 'there were served several bottles of The or tea ... This drink is made of the Herb The or Cha in fair water which afterwards they boil until a third part be consumed, to which they adde warm milk about a forth part, with a little salt, and then drink it as hot as they can well endure.' In France, Madame de Sévigné told a friend in a letter that she drank her tea with milk and recommended the beverage to her daughter, suggesting both milk and sugar.

In Britain the custom of adding milk to all types of tea was common by the middle of the 18th century and subsequently spread to the British colonies. The habit of course raises an important question – should the milk be poured into the tea or the tea into the milk? The answer depends on class, region, style of brewing and, of course, personal taste! Some will say that etiquette demands that the milk should be added to the tea and argue that it is more genteel and allows control of colour and strength, etc. (It is true that in the upper circles of Victorian society, poured cups of tea were handed to guests by the hostess or servants and the guests asked to help themselves to milk or cream and sugar.) Those in favour of 'milk in first' claim that this makes for a better mixing of the two fluids. There is also a belief that if cold milk is poured into boiling tea, there is a slight risk of spoiling the flavour of the brew by caramelizing the fat in the milk. Scientific experiments have in fact shown that this can happen and also that tiny globules of fat from the milk can remain floating on the surface of the cup of tea. But there is no easy answer to this point of debate and each individual tea-drinker must decide which method is best.

India

SIKKIM

DARJEELING

Siliguri

DOOARS

TERAI

ASSAM

Delhi

Lucknow

Guwahati

Bhopal

Calcutta

Bombay
(Mumbai)

Hyderabad

Madras

NILGIRI
Coonor
Coimbatore

Cochin

In the late 18th century, the tea plant was discovered growing as a native of Assam and the climate and altitude were declared to be suitable for tea cultivation. But it was not until 1834, after trials with the plant in Calcutta's botanical gardens, that commercial production started. The first plantings were made with seeds of the Chinese plant, the *Camellia sinensis*, and these did not thrive. Eventually, it was decided that the local *Camellia sinensis assamica* should be used instead and this enabled the plants to flourish. The first made Assam tea was shipped from India in 1838 and sold at the London Tea Auctions to declarations that it was every bit as good as tea from China. During the 1850s, the tea industry spread northwards up into Darjeeling and Bengal and then to Nilgiri in the beautiful Blue Mountains of India's south-western tip. Production increased rapidly from 183.4 tonnes in 1853 to 6,700 tonnes in 1870 and 35,274 tonnes in 1885. By 1947, when India won its independence from Britain, annual tea production stood at 281,089.6 tonnes. Since independence, the amount of land under tea has increased by 40% and production has gone up by 250%.

Today, India is one of the world's largest tea producers, with over 13,000 gardens and a workforce of more than 1.1 million employees who in turn generate income for a further 10 million people. India produces a mixture of orthodox and CTC black teas, many of which in the past were exported to Russia and Britain but which today are mostly consumed domestically. Some manufacturers concentrate on the production of CTC fannings and dust for the export teabag market, while others produce grainy CTC grades specifically for the home market. In 1993, 83% of production was of CTC teas. A small number of planters in the major growing regions prefer to offer high-quality, large-leaf orthodox teas to the connoisseur market both at home and abroad, and with a change in markets around the world and a shift in consumer tastes, are now also making green, white and oolong teas as well as the traditional speciality teas.

The Tea Board of India has worked consistently over the past few years to improve and maintain the reputation of teas from the country's three most important growing areas – Darjeeling, Assam and Nilgiri. Because of their consistently high quality, international demand for these teas has grown over the years and a situation had developed whereby teas were being misleadingly labelled and marketed as 'Pure Assam', 'Pure Darjeeling' and 'Pure Nilgiri', when in fact they were blended with teas from other countries and regions. In recent years, the Tea Board has been keen to ensure that all teas marketed as Assam, Darjeeling or Nilgiri genuinely contain 100% tea from those regions and has introduced a system of distinctive logos which, when displayed on the side of packets or tins, guarantees the genuine article. Teas from packers and blenders are regularly checked and certified by the Tea Board.

India

Assam, the 'land of the one-horned rhino', is a vast and beautiful area of dense forests and open rolling plains through which the mighty Brahmaputra river runs, carrying rich fertile soil down from the mountains of Tibet to the agricultural plains that stretch out on either side of the river. This is the largest tea-growing area in the world where, in 1993, almost 450,000 tonnes of tea were produced on 2,000 gardens – 53% of the all-India record crop of 835,552.7 tonnes. The average production today is 425,000 tonnes per year.

The Brahmaputra Valley shares borders with China, Burma and Bangladesh and although Assam teas are quite different from Darjeeling teas, the two areas lie only 120 miles apart. The rainfall in Assam is extremely high, usually between 200–300 centimetres (80–120 inches) per year but sometimes exceeding 10 metres (33 feet) in just one season. In one day, up to 30 centimetres (12 inches) of rain can fall, making the air heavy with humidity and the ground extremely wet. During the rainy season, the temperatures can rise to 100°C and on the plantations it is rather like being inside a vast glass greenhouse. The plants love these conditions and grow vigorously from spring to late autumn before the winter cold sends the bushes into their annual period of dormancy.

As in other major producing regions of the world, the Assam plantations and research centres have concentrated their efforts on producing cloned tea plants that can withstand drought, flooding, attacks by pests and disease, and which also offer an increased output of leaf. The leaf is made into both orthodox and CTC teas and then sold at the Guwuhati auctions, which mainly sell teas for the domestic market, or at the Siliguri and Calcutta auctions, which offer teas for export.

When the early spring weather in
March brings warmth to the
Brahmaputra Valley, the tea bushes begin to push out new leaf shoots and
are plucked to make Assam First Flush
teas. These are not considered to be
the best of Assam tea production and
are sold mainly for blending. However,
occasionally a good First Flush will be
offered as a single source speciality tea
and usually has a rich and fresh aroma
and flavour, though not the full malty
depth of a Second Flush.

Character
This tippy tea produces a mellow,
caramel-coloured tea with a long
smooth finish. It drinks well with
milk.

Brewing Tips
Infuse 2.5g in 200ml (7fl oz) water at
100°C (212°F) for 3–4 minutes.

India

Harmutty

The plucking of tea to make Second Flush Assams begins in June and continues through to September. The dry leaf of Second Flush Assams is characteristically a rich warm brown in colour with a good proportion of golden flecks mixed through it. These are the very tips of the new leaves, so new when picked that they do not contain the same proportion of tea chemicals as slightly larger leaves and so do not darken during the oxidation and drying period.

The high level of tippy leaves shows a carefully made, good-quality Assam tea. When the teas are brewed they give a warm coppery-coloured liquor and a rich, smooth, slightly sweet maltiness – a taste that is a favourite first thing in the morning and at breakfast.

Character
Large pieces of well-sorted tippy leaf that are a warm brown colour and flecked throughout with beautiful golden tips. The infusion is a wonderful mid-amber colour and the flavour is rich, sweet, malty and exquisitely smooth.

Brewing Tips
Brew 2.5g in 200ml (7fl oz) water at 100°C (212°F) for 4–5 minutes.

Fatikchera

As with all blends, the teas that make up the mixture are carefully selected from those available. The blend might include teas picked at different times of the season from the same garden; teas picked during the same season but from different gardens; or teas picked during different seasons from different gardens. The blend should always give the typical strong, malty richness expected from Assam teas. Blends can be of different grades and therefore may contain small or large leaves.

With a growing interest in green teas around the world, various regions of India are producing more and more green varieties. Assam greens tend to be light and delicate and have a slightly sweet aroma and flavour.

Character
Long fine pieces of green leaf that display a mixture of colours from pale jade to dark olive-brown. The pale amber infusion has a slightly grassy aroma and a lightly astringent flavour with citrus overtones.

Brewing Tips
Brew 2.5g in 200ml (7fl oz) water at 85°C (185°F) for 2–3 minutes.

The little hill town of Darjeeling nestles among the foothills of the snow-capped Himalayan mountains in the north-eastern corner of India. Commercial cultivation began here in the 1850s, when gardens were established at Tukvar, Aloobari and Steinthal. By 1866, there were 39 gardens producing 21,000 kilograms (46,300 pounds) of tea. By 1874 there were 113 gardens, with 6,000 hectares (14,800 acres) under tea.

Today, Darjeeling has 86 gardens planted out over an area of 19,000 hectares (47,000 acres) that produce over 10 million kilos (22 million pounds) every year. On the higher slopes, where altitudes reach 2,135 metres (7,000 feet), the Chinese variety of the tea plant is grown, since it withstands the intensely cold winters and the cool summer nights better than the Assam variety. But on the lower slopes, at altitudes of 915 metres (3,000 feet), the *Camellia sinensis assamica* grows quite happily in temperatures that are a little less harsh and where the air is a little more gentle. The unusual combination of high mountains, steep terrain, well-drained soil, extreme cold in winter and intense heat in summer, misty swirling clouds, a good level of well-distributed rainfall, and pure, clean mountain air produces the exquisite muscatel character and flowery aroma of good Darjeelings and which earns them the title, 'champagne' of Indian teas.

Because of the changing seasons, tea bushes in this part of India do not grow all year round. The bush is dormant from late November to early March and when the first rains have fallen and the first spring sunshine warmed the air, the bushes start growing again. The first new shoots, the First Flush, are picked during late March and April and produce teas that benefit from all the flavour and intensity stored in the bushes through the winter months. The Second Flush is picked in May and June. These teas have all the character of First Flush but tend to be more developed. The monsoon arrives in mid-June and drenches the area with roughly 3 metres (10 feet) of rain before September brings a drier season. Teas that grow during the monsoon period contain a high proportion of water, have the familiar character of Darjeeling teas but are less spectacular in flavour and aroma. Leaves that are gathered in the autumn months give a more mature flavour but are still aromatic and reminiscent of muscatel grapes.

First Flush Darjeelings are usually fresh, flowery, puckery, light and extremely aromatic. They are much sought after on world markets, win prizes at speciality food and drink events, and fetch very high prices at auction – sometimes more than £290 (500 US$) per kilo. Because of the variations in quality and character of teas from individual plantations each year, First Flush Darjeelings are sometimes treated rather like Beaujolais Nouveau and are flown in early, ahead of the normal shipments, for eager customers impatient to try the new season's teas. Many retailers now appreciate the fact that discerning customers enjoy making the comparison between Darjeelings from different gardens and different seasons, and so sell a range of teas from named gardens and specific harvests.

Goomtee is ranked each year among the top gardens in Darjeeling, along with Poobong, Thurbo, Castelton, Selimbong, Chamong and Margaret's Hope.

Character
Very green leaf showing colours ranging from bright light green to dark olive and oaky brown. The liquor is a pale greeny-amber colour, and has a deliciously sweet muscatel flavour with traditional winey overtones.

Brewing Tips
Brew 2.5g in 200ml (7fl oz) water at 82°C (180°F) for 3 minutes.

India

Poobong

Tong Song

Located in the Ghoom area of
Darjeeling, this prized garden (whose
name in ancient Tibetan means 'valleys
beyond the clouds') produces some of
the finest Darjeeling teas.

Character
Made with leaves gathered from
bushes that originated in China, this
tea is more full-bodied than most First
Flush Darjeelings. It gives a rich amber-coloured infusion with a complex
bouquet and a definite note of green
muscat.

Brewing Tips
Brew 2.5g in 200ml (7fl oz) water at
100°C (212°F) for 3–4 minutes.

Second Flush Darjeelings are made
from teas plucked in May and June.
Since the bushes have been steadily
strengthening as the year progresses,
the flavour of the teas is slightly more
developed than that of First Flush teas.
Many people prefer the slightly more
mature character of these teas and
consider them the best that Darjeeling
produces.

Character
Mainly brown leaf mingled with hints
of olive green and gold to give a pale
amber cup with a sweet honey-like
flavour.

Brewing Tips
Brew 2.5g in
200ml (7fl oz)
water at 100°C
(212°F) for 3 minutes.

During the monsoon summer months the heavy rains give teas that are of a more ordinary quality and character than First and Second Flush. Then, in the autumn, after the monsoon, come the autumnal teas. The autumnals have the Darjeeling character but give a darker, amber-coloured liquor that has a smoother, more rounded, mature flavour and a little more body compared to the teas made earlier in the year.

Since some tea-drinkers like to enjoy the same flavour when they brew their preferred Darjeeling, packers and blenders usually offer a Darjeeling blend that has all the characteristic light, slightly astringent, almost grape-like flavour of the variety but does not vary from season to season or from year to year. The carefully balanced blend may contain teas from one or several different gardens in the Darjeeling region.

Character
Mixed colour leaf displaying pieces that are bright green through to deep jade and brown. The infusion is greeny-brown and has a pronounced sweet muscatel aroma and a gentle, lightly fruity flavour.

Brewing Tips
Brew 2.5g in 200ml (7fl oz) water at 100°C (212°F) for 3–4 minutes.

India

Poobong

Poobong

Character
A bud and two new leaves are picked to make a tea that looks similar to Chinese Bai Mudan. The buds remain silvery while the surrounding leaves are a mixture of sage green and brown. The infusion is pale greeny-yellow, the aroma has a hint of lemon and the flavour is very light and slightly citrus.

Brewing Tips
Brew 2.5g in 200ml (7fl oz) water at 85°C (180°F) for 5–6 minutes.

Character
This is a mixture of small silvery-green buds that are just beginning to unfurl and leaves that are a little more developed. Breathing in the aroma from the honey-coloured liquor is like burying one's nose in a bunch of very ripe muscatel grapes. The flavour is soft, light and very velvety.

Brewing Tips
Brew 2.5g in 200ml (7fl oz) water at 82°C (180°F) for 2–3 minutes.

Selim Hill

Kamala

Character
Large, slightly twisted, dark greeny-brown leaf. The jade green infusion has an aroma that reminds you of the seashore and the lightly astringent, herby flavour is round and full in the mouth.

Brewing Tips
Brew 2.5g in 200ml (7fl oz) water at 85°C (180°F) for 2–3 minutes.

Tea production started in the Dooars region in the 1860s in a small area lying amongst the Himalayan foothills, just west of Assam and just south of Darjeeling, and where little hill streams run down through the tea plantations that cover the gently sloping hillsides all around. The teas grown here are typically dark and full-bodied but have less character than Assam teas.

Character
The leaf of this typical orthodox Dooars tea is a mixture of pale sage green and pale golden-brown. The infusion is the colour of whisky and has a light flavour with a hint of astringency.

Brewing Tips
Brew 2.5g in 200ml (7fl oz) water at 100°C (212°F) for 3–4 minutes.

India

Dunsandle FOP Organic

Some 1,500 miles south of Darjeeling and Assam, India's southern tea plantations stretch through the range of the Nilgiri Hills or 'Blue Mountains' that run down the south-western tip of the country from Kerala to Tamil Nadu. In 1840, the first British planter, Colonel John Ouchterlony, and his brother James decided to establish tea plantations in the midst of stunningly beautiful, rolling grasslands and dense jungles where eucalyptus trees, cypresses and blue gum trees grow and elephants roam free. With its high elevations and approximately 200 centimetres (80 inches) of rainfall every year, Nilgiri is an extremely suitable location and today there are roughly 25,000 hectares (62,000 acres) of land under tea, growing at altitudes of between 300 and 1,800 metres (1,000 and 6,000 feet) above sea level. Every slope, valley and plateau is covered with tea bushes which grow steadily throughout the year. Although the new shoots are plucked all year, the two most important harvesting periods are in April and May, when approximately 25% of the crop is picked, and again from September to December, when a further 35–40% of the annual crop is gathered. The teas produced here are flavoury, bright and brisk, often with a similar character to the Ceylon teas that grow to the east on the island of Sri Lanka. The majority of Nilgiri's teas are used in blending but more and more are now marketed as single source teas.

Situated in the lofty mountains of the famous Nilgiri Highlands, the Dunsandle FOP Organic estate overlooks the Indian Ocean.

Character
This bright, fragrant tea is possibly one of the few teas left in South India with all the character, flavour and appearance of a traditionally produced orthodox Nilgiri. The larger leaf contains some tips and brews a light amber-coloured infusion that has a delicate, slightly fruity flavour.

Brewing Tips
Brew 2.5g in 200ml (7fl oz) water at 100°C (212°F) for 3–4 minutes.

Burnside Frost

Temi

Character
The contrasting leaf has a distinctive aroma and flavour profile. Flagrantly fragrant, it is a high-grown black tea with an appetizing greenness to its flavour.

Brewing Tips
Infuse 3.5g in 200ml (7fl oz) water at 100°C (212°F) for 4–5 minutes.

Sikkim is a small tea-growing area on the eastern side of the Himalayan mountains, to the north of Darjeeling and bordering Tibet, Nepal and Bhutan. Its dramatic mountain peaks, lush green valleys and cascading rivers create a breathtaking backdrop for the tea bushes. The only tea plantation is Temi, established in 1969 on an area of approximately 160 hectares (400 acres), and the teas produced here are similar in character to Darjeelings but more full-bodied and fruity.

Character
The greeny-brown leaves are beautifully twisted with plenty of golden tip and give a powerful, sweet fruity aroma and a deliciously fragrant, almost honey-like flavour.

Brewing Tips
Brew 2.5g in 200ml (7fl oz) water at 93°C (200°F) for 2 minutes.

India

WHAT'S IN TEA?

The leaves of the *Camellia sinensis* contain a number of chemicals (including amino-acids, carbohydrates, mineral ions, caffeine and polyphenolic compounds) that give tea its characteristic colour and flavour. They also contain 75–80% water, which is reduced, during the first withering stages, to 60–70%. The firing or drying process deactivates the enzyme that causes oxidation and reduces the water content to approximately 3%.

During oxidation, polyphenolic flavanols (or catechins) react with oxygen to create the unique flavour and colour of the infused liquor. The aroma of tea is extremely complex and so far more than 550 chemicals have been identified in the aroma of black tea. These include hydrocarbons, alcohols and acids, most of which are formed during the manufacturing process and which add their own qualities to the flavour and aroma of the tea. However, the taste mainly results from the various polyphenolic compounds (often incorrectly called tannins) being modified by caffeine. Both black and green teas contain similar amounts of polyphenols (flavanoids), although quantities vary in different types of tea. Green tea contains simple flavanoids called catechins while oolong and black teas contain more complex flavanoids called theaflavins and thearubigins. These flavanoids act as antioxidants in the body and help work against the effects of 'free radicals', which are found in the air that we breathe, in cigarette smoke, in sunlight, etc., and which are thought to cause age-related diseases such heart disease and cancer. Although tannins are present in tea, this does not mean that tea contains tannic acid, as is often assumed.

The caffeine content of tea acts as a mild stimulant and helps increase the activity of the digestive system and the kidneys, as well as raising general alertness, improving performance and combating tiredness. All types of tea contain caffeine but the amounts vary according to the manufacturing process. White and green teas have the least caffeine, oolong has a little more and black teas have the most. And yet a cup of black tea contains only about 50mg caffeine – less than a third of the amount found in a 190ml (6½fl oz) cup of filter coffee. Those people who do not wish to take caffeine into their bodies should therefore choose a very light white or green tea or a herbal infusion that contains no caffeine at all. Tea also contains traces of calcium, zinc, potassium, manganese, Vitamins B1, B2, B6 and B12, folate, niacin, and pantothenate.

Japan

Nagano

Tokyo

Kyoto

Hiroshima

SHIKOKU

Nagasaki

KYUSHU

In the early days of cultivation in Japan, tea was plucked by hand. Today, however, almost all tea is harvested by machine. The disadvantage of mechanical harvesting is that the machine cannot tell the difference between tender new leaf buds and shoots and older, tougher stems and leaves. The Japanese method of gathering the leaves also gives plantations in Japan a different appearance from those in other parts of the world. The bushes are planted side by side in long rows, creating waves of green across the gently rolling countryside, and as the machines are guided over the top of the bushes, so a curved 'plucking table' develops. (In regions where bushes are picked by hand, the plucking table is much flatter). Whereas in most tea-growing countries a certain amount of manual work is still involved, the Japanese tea industry is mechanized throughout the entire manufacturing process – from picking and steaming the leaves to rolling, drying, sorting and packing.

The Japanese growing areas are all in hilly parts of the country close to rivers, streams and lakes where the climate is misty and damp and the amount of hot sunshine is tempered by cooler, hazy mornings and softer light. The harvest begins at the end of April and between two and four crops are gathered each year before the late autumn weather brings a period of dormancy. Only green teas are produced and the varieties vary according to the time of year the leaves are picked, the part of the plant used and the manufacturing method employed.

Gyokuro

Gyokuro is Japan's most expensive, highest quality tea and it is grown, picked and processed with extreme care and skill. The bushes are kept under 90% shade for about 20 days prior to harvesting. Just as the new leaf buds start to form, the bushes are covered with bamboo, reed or canvas mats and the reduced light forces the plant to produce a higher concentration of chlorophyl and darker green leaves.

Character
The neat flat needles are a deep rich green flecked with hints of yellow and paler green. The infusion is clear pale yellow and the aroma and flavour sweet, mild and very smooth.

Brewing Tips
Brew 9g in 80ml (3fl oz) water at 60°C (140°F) for 2–3 minutes. Strain and drink and add more water for a further infusion.

Japan

Matcha

Matcha, the very fine green powdered tea used for the Japanese Tea Ceremony, is made by grinding Tencha, a finely chopped tea made in the same way as Gyokuro. Before the leaves are gathered, the bushes are shaded in the same way as for Gyokuro and then slightly larger leaves are harvested, steamed and dried but are not rolled. Instead the veins and stems are removed and the remaining leaf parts are ground to a very fine powder. To prepare this for the Tea Ceremony, the powder is whisked into hot water with a specially crafted bamboo whisk.

Character
The finely ground powder is a vibrant lime green. When whisked into hot water, the tea dissolves, giving a thin, frothy, intensely green drink that has a distinctive grassy flavour.

Brewing Tips
Warm a bowl and a whisk with hot water, then tip the water away. Measure two thirds of a teaspoon of Matcha into the bowl and gently pour in 60ml (2fl oz) water at 80°C (175°F), and whisk briskly to make a foamy liquid.

Kukicha is made from the stems and stalks that are removed from the leaves used in the production of Sencha, Gyokuro and Tencha. The higher the quality of the stalks and stems, the finer the flavour of the tea. The highest quality tea made from the stems of Gyokuro is known as 'karigane'.

Character
The tea is a mixture of dark green leaves and stalky, fibrous, straw-coloured pieces. The infusion is pale yellowy-green and it has a light fragrance and a clean, sweet, almost nutty flavour.

Brewing Tips
Brew 7g in 240ml (8.5fl oz) water at 90°C (194°F) for 30–60 seconds. Strain and drink and add more water for a second infusion.

Japan

Sencha

Sencha is made from the first picking of the leaves in spring. The freshly picked leaves are steamed (in order to de-enzyme the tea and enhance the green colour), followed by alternate drying and rolling. Sencha has a high vitamin C content.

Character
The long, flat, emerald green needles of tea are flecked with hints of pale green and give a light golden-yellow infusion. The delicately sweet aroma and flavour are reminiscent of freshly mown grass and sea breezes.

Brewing Tips
Brew 6g in 160ml (5.5fl oz) water at 80°C (175°F) for 2 minutes. Strain and drink and add more water for a second infusion.

Bancha is made from the summer and autumn picking of the leaves when the stalks and leaves are tougher and coarser than those gathered earlier in the year to make Sencha. Bancha is less fine and delicate in taste but has a high fluoride content and is therefore considered to be beneficial to the health of the teeth.

Character
Bancha has a coarser appearance than Sencha and is more yellow-green in colour. The infusion is a deeper golden-yellow and the aroma and flavour stronger, more astringent and less fragrant.

Brewing Tips
Brew 4.5g in 200ml (7fl oz) water at 100°C (212°F) for 15–30 seconds.

Japan

Houjicha

Houjicha is made by roasting Sencha or Bancha. The idea of roasting green leaves was invented in 1920 by a Kyoto merchant who had a surplus stock of old green leaves which he did not want to waste.

Character
The leaves are toasty brown and have a sweet, biscuity smell. The infusion is rich amber in colour and has a mild, slightly savoury aroma and flavour.

Brewing Tips
Brew 4.5g in 200ml (7fl oz) water at 100°C (212°F) for 15–30 seconds.

Genmaicha

To make this popular tea, hulled rice kernels and popped corn are mixed with Bancha or medium-grade Sencha.

Character
The mixture of tea and grains gives a bright golden liquor that has a nutty, slightly savoury aroma and flavour.

Brewing Tips
Brew 4.5g in 200ml (7fl oz) water at 100°C (212°F) for 15–30 seconds.

Kenya

SUDAN

ETHIOPIA

UGANDA

•Kitale

•Isiolo

▲ *Mount Kenya*

SOMALI
REPUBLIC

■Nairobi

Masai
Mara
National
Reserve

•Mombasa

TANZANIA

INDIAN
OCEAN

Tea was first planted in Kenya in 1903 when white settlers experimented with a few tea bushes at Limuru in Kiambu District. Production slowly increased in the Kenya Highlands of Kericho and Nandi, and in 1950 the Tea Board of Kenya was established in order to oversee what was becoming an important cash crop for the country. In 1964, the Kenya Tea Development Authority (KTDA) was founded with the objective of promoting and supporting the cultivation of tea by smallholder farmers in suitable areas of the country.

The main growing region is in the Kenya Highlands where plantations lie at altitudes ranging from 1,520 to 2,750 metres (5,000 to 9,000 feet) and where copious rainfall encourages the bushes to grow vigorously throughout the year. Whereas most of Kenya is too dry for tea cultivation, this mountain region benefits from the humidity that rises from Lake Victoria and falls as rain over the Highlands. The Kenyan bushes flush all year but the best crops are harvested from late January to July.

In the 1960s, only one factory was processing the picked tea but today the KTDA manages 51 factories and others are under construction. These factories together have a processing capacity of more than 15,000 tonnes of green leaf. Most companies manufacture CTC teas for teabag blends but some orthodox teas are still made and are reaching growing markets

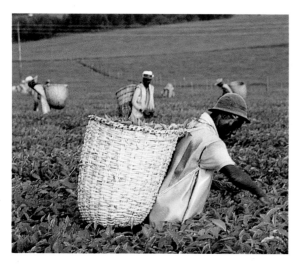

around the world. At Kangaita Tea Estate, clonal tea plants have been carefully selected to produce an excellent selection of large-leafed teas. Connoisseurs can now choose from Mount Kenya OP, Simba BOPF, Muthaiga FP, Aberdares FOP, or Nakuru BOP made at Kangaita Tea Factory. Marinyn Tea Estate also still produces a small amount of orthodox tea in the Rift Valley between Mount Kenya and Lake Victoria.

Kangaita OP

Grown on plantations owned by the Kenya Tea Development Agency, these high-quality black teas are now reaching a niche speciality market around the world.

Character
Neat browny-black leaf that gives a warm dark amber infusion and has a satisfying, warm aroma and a smooth but powerful flavour.

Brewing Tips
Infuse 2.5g in 200ml (7fl oz) water at 100°C (212°F) for 4–5 minutes.

Kenya BOP Blend

Small-leafed Kenya teas are often used to give strength and colour to breakfast blends but they also drink well alone. They are especially good with rich chocolate foods.

Character
Dark brown small leaf that gives a rich red liquor and has a good, strong, balanced flavour.

Brewing Tips
Infuse 2.5g in 200ml (7fl oz) water at 100°C (212°F) for 2–3 minutes.

wet leaf

Kenya

TEAS THROUGH THE DAY

The wide variety of teas available today means that each individual tea-drinker can choose something to suit the palate, time of day, food being served, mood, season, weather. Everyone has a favourite early-morning tea, a tea to drink by the fire on a dark and dismal winter afternoon, an evening tea to enjoy after a wonderful dinner. There are no firm rules as to which tea should be drunk when, but here are some guidelines:

FIRST THING IN THE MORNING AND AT BREAKFAST choose a strong black tea that gives a gentle dose of caffeine and helps get the brain and body going, such as English Breakfast, Irish Breakfast, Assam, Kenya or Yunnan. These have a strength and depth that will marry well with the strong flavours of cooked breakfast foods, and with breads and pastries served with preserves or honey.

MID-MORNING AND AT LUNCHTIME choose a tea that will continue to help you concentrate and perform well through the working day. Any of the morning teas work well, or choose smoky Lapsang Souchong, flavoury Ceylon, China Keemun or Nilgiri. If lunch consists of oriental food, choose a green Sencha or Chinese Chun Mee or Gunpowder.

AS THE AFTERNOON PROGRESSES turn to lighter teas that offer a fragrance and gentleness to soothe and calm – perhaps a peachy oolong, a fruity Darjeeling, a lighter Ceylon, any variety of green tea, or a flavoured tea such as mango or peach.

AT AFTERNOON TEA choose teas that pair well with the food offered. Earl Grey goes extremely well with cheese sandwiches or savouries, and with lemon cake or lemon tarts; Darjeeling is excellent with anything creamy so is perfect with scones and clotted cream; Lapsang Souchong is wonderful with smoked salmon or smoked chicken sandwiches; a brisk Ceylon enhances fresh fruit or sandwiches made with cucumber, tomatoes and other salad ingredients; strong Kenya and English Breakfast blends are great with chocolate cakes, rich truffles and chocolate cheesecakes.

IN THE EVENING perfect teas are the lighter oolongs, greens and whites. These have less caffeine and offer an elegance and cleanness that is good after dinner and before sleep. These are also teas that drink well alone, without food, and create just the right mood for the time of day when life begins to slow down.

Malawi

Chitipa

Kaporo

TANZANIA

ZAMBIA

Lake Malawi

MOZAMBIQUE

Chipata

Lilongwe

Monkey Bay

MOZAMBIQUE

Mwanze

▲ *Mount Mulanje*

Mulanje

Tea cultivation started in Malawi in 1878 when tea seeds were taken from the Royal Botanic Gardens in Edinburgh and planted in land that was then called Nyasaland. When plantations were established in the lowlands of Mulanje and Thyolo in the Shire Highlands, the seeds used came from Natal in South Africa where plants had originally been transplanted from Ceylon. Unpredictable weather patterns can make tea-growing difficult for the Malawi planters but the introduction of more clonal plants has helped ease this problem. Malawi was in fact the first African country to introduce clonal methods of estate refurbishment.

The main picking season is during Malawi's summer from October to April, when plenty of rain encourages the bushes to flush continuously. Today, Malawi exports more than 35,000 tonnes every year and, after Kenya, is Africa's second most important tea-producing country. All the teas are CTC blacks and are valued for their wonderful bright colour and rich flavour that adds quality to both teabag and loose-leaf blends.

Kavusi

Character
Small leaf that gives a rich coppery in-fusion with a strong, pungent flavour. Drinks well with a little milk.

Brewing Tips
Brew 2.5g in 200ml (7fl oz) water at 100°C (212°F) for 3 minutes.

Namingomba

Character
Good-quality, pure clonal, small-leafed tea that gives a coppery red infusion and a full-bodied flavour. Drinks well with milk.

Brewing Tips
Infuse 2.5g in 200ml (7fl oz) water at 100°C (212°F) for 3 minutes.

Malawi

TEA-LEAF READING

For hundreds of years, the art of tea-leaf reading has fascinated and entranced tea-drinkers. Many people believe that the wet tea leaves scattered in the cup after the tea has been drunk are as good a guide to future events as the reading of palms and tarot cards.

Tasseology is an intuitive art married with psychic skills that enables the reader to see into the future. As leading tasseologist Amber McCarroll says in her book, *The Magic in Tea Leaves*, 'universal symbolism … acts as a pictorial shorthand for the subconscious and we can all benefit from developing this forgotten skill'. The information gained from a tea-leaf reading usually applies only to the 24 hours immediately following the reading and for the best results, the reader must only look for answers to specific questions. A reading is only relevant to whoever has drunk from the cup.

• To prepare the cup, make a pot of tea in the usual way. Larger leaves are best as they create a more revealing mixture of images and patterns.
• Pour a cup of tea without using a strainer, so that some of the leaves go into the cup with the liquor.
• Drink the tea in the usual way but leave about a teaspoonful of liquid in the bottom of the cup with the leaves.

The drinker then holds the cup in the left hand with the rim upwards and turns it fast three times in an anti-clockwise direction. The drinker tips the cup onto a saucer and allows the tea to drain into the saucer before turning the cup the right way up again and handing it to the reader.

The reader holds the cup with the handle pointing towards the body and tries to interpret the significance of the leaves, and so help the drinker relate the pattern to specific aspects of their life – and to the specific question being asked. Leaves scattered near the handle represent personal and home life. Leaves to the left of the handle represent the past and leaves to the right indicate the future. Those on the opposite side of the cup represent far-off events and people, while those in the bottom are to do with difficult emotions. The area around the rim signifies happy times and positive events and the ring that runs halfway around the inside of the cup is connected with everyday emotions and events. The reader focuses on a particular area of the cup according to the nature of the question being asked.

Nepal

While on a tour of Darjeeling in 1873, Colonel Gajraj Singh Thapa tasted the tea there and was so impressed that he determined to cultivate the plant in Nepal, where he was Governor-general. He established two plantations at Ilam and Soktim where the first Nepalese orthodox teas were produced. In 1985, five eastern regions of the country – Jhapa, Ilam, Panchthar, Terhathum and Dhankuta – were declared a 'tea-zone' by the government and since then three new plantations and seven new factories have been established. Since 1920, the land area under tea has increased from 94 hectares (233 acres) to 810 hectares (2,000 acres), and produc-

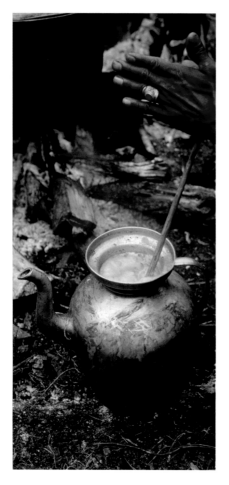

tion has increased from 2 tonnes to 1,000 tonnes. The gardens are situated at altitudes ranging from 915 metres (3,000 feet) to 1,830 metres (6,000 feet) above sea level and the plants grown are mostly of the China variety, as this more easily withstands the mountains' cold temperatures. The teas, which are all black, are grown on approximately 5,000 family smallholdings and 100 or so larger gardens and estates, and processed in 16 CTC and 11 orthodox factories. After a period of dormancy in the icy winter months, the first new shoots begin to appear in late February and are gathered through to April to make the First Flush, which gives a pale golden-coloured liquor and a soft, delicate flavour. In May and June, the Second Flush is gathered to give a slightly more mature tea that has a fuller taste and a fruity character. From mid-June to the end of September, the region is drenched by the monsoon rains and the teas made during this season have a higher water content, a darker colour and stronger flavour. October's autumn teas have a much richer aroma and a marked muscatel flavour.

Character

The leaves of this exquisite tea are blackish-brown with lots of tip. The tea brews to an amber cup and has a woody aroma and a clean, refreshing, sweet floral flavour, similar to Darjeeling.

Brewing Tips

Brew 2.5g in 200ml (7fl oz) water at 100°C (212°F) for 3–4 minutes.

Character

The leaves are a mixture of silver, green and brown with a scattering of golden tips. The infusion is a clear pale honey colour and has a soft, slightly nutty aroma and flavour.

Brewing Tips

Brew 2.5g in 200ml (7fl oz) water at 100°C (212°F) for 3–4 minutes.

Nepal

NAMING THE DRINK

In English, it is *tea*, but once upon a time, it was *tee* or *tay*. In India it is *cha* or *chai*. How did the different words develop?

The form of the name that entered each language depended on the route by which tea was first traded into that country. When tea first travelled outside China to the Arab countries and Russia, the Mandarin word, *cha*, spread with the goods. In Persian, Japanese and Hindi, the word settled as *cha*, in Arabic, *shai*, in Tibetan, *ja*, in Turkish, *chay* and in Russian, *chai*.

When the Portuguese first started buying tea from the Chinese, they traded through the port of Macao where the Mandarin word for tea had become *ch'a* in the locally spoken Cantonese. But Dutch tea ships sailed in and out of the port of Amoy in China's Fujian Province and so used the local Amoy word *te*, pronounced 'tay', and changed it to *thee*. As it was the Dutch who were mainly responsible for trading tea to other European countries and beyond, the oriental beverage became known as *tea* or *tee* in English; *thé* in French; *thee* in German; *té* in Italian, Spanish, Danish, Norwegian, Hungarian, and Malay; *tee* in Finnish; *tey* in Tamil; *thay* in Singhalese; and *Thea* to scientists.

OTHER USES FOR TEA

Rinse **auburn or brown hair** with tea to bring out the red lights … Relieve tired **eyes** by laying used, wet teabags over the eyelids for 15 minutes … Soothe tired **feet** by soaking them for half an hour in a bowl filled with warm or cold weak tea … Ease the sting of **sunburn** with a solution of cold tea … Tip used wet tea leaves and any cold tea left in the pot on the soil around **rose** and **camellia bushes** … Pour unwanted cold tea onto the soil in which **house plants** grow … **Dye** fabrics to a soft browny-fawn colour by soaking in a solution of hot tea … Soak a cloth in cold tea, wring it out and use to wipe over **wood** surfaces and lacquer work … Soak **dried fruits** in cold tea before adding to a cake mix.

Sri Lanka

INDIA

Jaffna

Trincomalee

Anuradhapura

●Sigiriya

●Kandy

●Nuwara Eliya

Colombo ▲ *Adam's Peak*

Galle

Tangalla

Until the 1860s, the main crop grown on the teardrop-shaped island of Ceylon was coffee, but when the coffee-rust fungus brought devastation to the estates in 1869, planters were forced to diversify if they were to avoid total ruin. At Loolecondera Estate, tea had been considered as an alternative as early as the 1850s and in 1866 the owners chose James Taylor, a tough, determined and extremely hard-working Scot, to oversee the first sowings of tea seeds on the plantation. With some basic knowledge that he had acquired in India, Taylor started manufacturing black tea on the veranda of his bungalow, rolling the leaf by hand and drying the oxidized leaf in clay stoves heated over charcoal fires. After the success of the first teas, a fully equipped factory was set up in 1872 and the first Ceylon teas

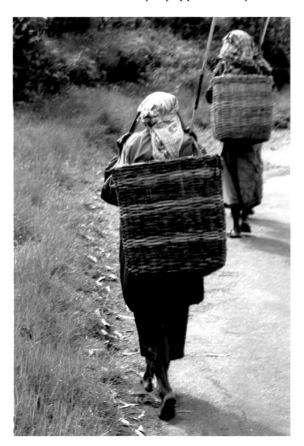

were shipped to England and sold at the London auctions in 1873. From those experimental beginnings, the Ceylon tea industry grew rapidly, with production increasing from 23 pounds of tea in 1880 to nearly 23 tonnes in 1890. In 1883, the first Ceylon tea auction was held in the capital Colombo by a company called Mssrs. Sommerville & Co. The auctions today handle almost 6,000 tonnes of tea every week, making Colombo the world's largest auction centre. Exports from the island have increased from 215,000 tonnes in 1990 to 288,000 tonnes in 2000, a growth of 34%.

In 1993, with a growing demand worldwide for small-leafed teas suitable for the teabag market, the government encouraged producers (by offering financial incentives) to convert from orthodox to CTC manufacturing, but the experiment was not a success and 40 or so factories have now returned to orthodox production. The CTC factories that operate today are mostly in the low-grown areas and are enjoying increasing support from international buyers who seek good-quality teas for teabag manufacture. Some producers have now entered the 'value added' market by packing flavoured teas, loose teas and teabags at the factory rather than exporting their teas in bulk, and others have started producing green and organic teas to meet a changing world market. After a decade of problems and uncertainty, the industry has gained a new level of stability, with increasing orders from important markets in the former Soviet Union, the UAE, Syria, Turkey, Iran, Saudi Arabia, Iraq, Egypt, Japan and the UK.

Sri Lanka's plantations are situated at elevations of between 460 and 2,450 metres (1,500 and 8,000 feet) in the central southern part of the island. There are six main growing areas – Ratnapura, a low-growing area about 55 miles east of the capital Colombo; Galle, a low-growing region situated in the south of the country; Kandy, the low-growing area around the ancient capital, where the first plantations were established; Dimbula, a mid- to high-growing region west of the central mountains; Uva, also a mid- to high-growing area that lies to the west of Dimbula; and Nuwara Eliya, the highest tea region, which produces some of the very finest of Ceylon teas.

The leaf is plucked all year round, with the best teas being made in January and February. The teas give a typically smooth, bright liquor, a delicate perfume and a rich golden flavour. In the hot and humid foothills, the bushes flush every seven or eight days. Each area has its own weather patterns and geographic features and it is these that give the individual teas their characteristic flavours and aromas. Low-grown teas are of good quality but sometimes lack the brisk, bright flavour of the higher-grown teas and so are more often used in blending. The mid-grown teas have greater richness and strength and give good colour, while the high-grown teas are considered to be the best of Sri Lanka's production, giving a beautiful golden infusion and a powerful intensity of flavour.

DIMBULA

Kirkoswold

GALLE

Lumbini Estate

The important growing area of Dimbula covers the western slopes of the island's tea-growing region. The monsoon brings torrential rain during August and September and the best teas are gathered from December to March/April. The teas produced here are noted for their body and strength and wonderful aroma and vary through the season from full bodied to lighter and more fragrant.

Character
The leaves from this award-winning estate yield a coppery-coloured cup with golden notes and a full-bodied flavour.

Brewing Tips
Brew 2.5g in 200ml (7fl oz) water at 100°C (212°F) for 4 minutes.

The teas from the low-growing region of Galle in the south of the island are noted for their large, very black leaf, stylish appearance and the high level of golden and silvery tips. The success of the teas has led to an increase in the number of small private planters growing tea here.

Character
This tea gives a very rich, strong and smooth infusion that has the smoky overtones of a China black. It drinks well with milk.

Brewing Tips
Brew 2.5g in 200ml (7fl oz) water at 100°C (212°F) for 4 minutes.

Lovers' Leap

New Vithanakande

The tea from Nuwara Eliya, Sri Lanka's highest tea-growing region, is often referred to as Sri Lanka's 'champagne of teas' and is sought after by tea-drinkers all over the world. The best teas of the area give a beautiful, golden liquor that is light, smooth and bright, and has an exquisite perfume.

Character
The brisk caramel liquor has a flowery aroma and a light flavour that is wonderful to drink after dinner.

Brewing Tips
Brew 2.5g in 200ml (7fl oz) water at 100°C (212°F) for 4–5 minutes.

The tea gardens in the south-western, low-growing Ratnapura region are protected from the drying winds of the south-western monsoon by the forest belt of the Sinharaja Forest Reserve that lies just to the south. The teas produced here are full bodied, thick and strong.

Character
The beautifully tippy, wiry leaves produce a bright amber cup that has a distinctive aroma and a smooth caramel finish.

Brewing Tips
Infuse 2.5g in 200ml (7fl oz) water at 100°C (212°F) for 4–5 minutes.

Uva St James's Estate BOP

Uva OP

The teas from the high eastern slopes of the central mountains in the Uva district have a unique flavour and pungency, caused mainly by the 'Cachan' wind that blows in from the north east at the end of July until mid-August. During this period, the leaves of the tea bushes close up to protect themselves from the harsh drying effect of the wind, so flavour is concentrated in a way that does not happen at other times of the year. Local factories concentrate on making Broken Orange Pekoe and Broken Orange Pekoe fannings, to make the most of the intense flavour.

Character
The copper-coloured infusion has a smooth, pronounced taste and a wonderful aroma. It drinks well with milk.

Brewing Tips
Brew 2.5g in 200ml (7fl oz) water at 100°C (212°F) for 4 minutes.

Character
The neat dark brown leaf is mingled with a few golden flecks of tip. The clear infusion is a beautiful dark amber colour and has an aroma that is reminiscent of warm woodland. The flavour is sweet and mild and intensely satisfying.

Brewing Tips
Brew 2.5g in 200ml (7fl oz) water at 100°C (212°F) for 3–4 minutes.

Character
Down-covered buds yield a light flowery liquor that has a sweet finish.

Brewing Tips
Brew 2.5g in 200ml (7fl oz) water at 82°C (180°F) for 4–7 minutes. Strain and add more water for three further infusions.

Many companies create blends for their customers to offer a characteristic brisk golden Ceylon flavour and colour. Orange Pekoe and Broken Orange Pekoe blends are the most popular and a well-balanced tea will give a rich, golden liquor and a fresh, bright, taste, sometimes with a hint of lemon.

Sri Lanka

TEA AND HEALTH

When tea was first drunk in Ancient China, it was considered to possess health-promoting properties and, as well as being drunk after meals as an aid to digestion, it was used in ointments and skin creams. When tea arrived in Europe, it was sold by apothecaries and advertised as a tonic brew that had the power to cure stomach complaints, skin disorders, headaches, fevers, loss of memory, sleepiness and many other everyday ailments. Today, some Chinese tea dealers give helpful suggestions on their packaging as to what each tea is good for – for example, Leo Kwan of the Ming Cha Tea Company tells his customers that Silver Needles tea (Yin Zhen) is good for 'cooling of body heat, purification of the blood pertaining to the effects of abnormal heat …'.

Until the 20th century, few of the health claims made on behalf of tea had been proved, but recent research around the world and coordinated studies have given us more and more evidence that tea does indeed have many tangible health benefits. We now know that tea contains polyphenols that have an antioxidant effect in the body and can help protect us against certain age-related and degenerative diseases. These antioxidant effects have been compared to those of certain fruits and vegetables. One study concluded that drinking three cups of tea a day was equivalent to eating six apples. In the case of heart disease and stroke, reports indicate that tea can help reduce the inflammation connected with atherosclerosis and vascular problems. Tea polyphenols have also been shown to inhibit the development of cancer cells. Studies with animals have revealed that tea flavonoids can help protect against skin cancer, lung cancer and digestive cancer in mice and rats.

Studies in a number of different countries indicate that tea is also helpful in reducing blood cholesterol, and it is thought that puerh and oolong teas are particularly beneficial.

Tea also aids good dental health, as the polyphenolic components in tea have the effect of helping to reduce the formation of plaque and bacteria in the mouth while the fluoride content strengthens tooth enamel and helps reduce the development of cavities. Green tea contains twice as much fluoride as black. In China and Japan toothpaste is now made containing a certain amount of tea extract.

Taiwan

CHINA

Hsinchu

Taipei

Hsueshan

Tienhsiang

*Jade Mountain
(Yushan)*

Alishan

Tainan

The cultivation of tea bushes in Formosa (as Taiwan was formerly named) began some two hundred years ago when Chinese migrants from the mainland province of Fukien settled here and brought with them their tea-making skills. The soil, climate and hilly landscape were found to be perfect for the tea plant and in 1869 Englishman John Dodd was responsible for exporting the first Taiwan-made tea from the island when he hired two clippers to sail the teas to New York. By the 1880s, Formosa was famous for its teas and was annually exporting more than 10 million pounds.

Although early cultivation was concentrated mainly around T'ai-Pei, most of the central region of the island now produces very high-quality green, oolong and black teas. The plantations are all above 305 metres (1,000 feet) and cover a total area of some 21,223 hectares (52,468 acres). The teas are grown on family-owned 'boutique tea farms' where the owner/tea master oversees the entire process and passes his or her skills and secret methods of manufacture on to the next generation so that the production of prized teas can continue. The small farms are controlled by local collectives who make sure that standards remain high.

The bush flushes five times between April and December and the finest quality teas are made from leaf gathered from the end of May to the middle of August. Leaves for the premium grades are gathered in the early part of the afternoon, between noon and 4 o'clock, and the pickers are carefully chosen for their years of experience, meaning their nimble fingers know exactly which leaves to pick. Different types of tea are made in different parts of the island and the most famous today are the wonderful high-altitude oolongs from the Lishan, Tung Ting and Wenshan mountains. These tend to be more flowery and sweeter than oolongs from China and the lower-grown Formosa oolongs. They sell at very high prices both in the domestic market and abroad, sometimes fetching $600–$700 per pound.

Formosa Gunpowder

Tung Ting

The leaves used to make Gunpowder are carefully selected for quality, size and style. They are then tightly rolled into large pellets.

Character
As the little nuggets of leaf absorb water and slowly uncurl, they release a strong, dark green infusion with a memorable aroma and a slightly grassy, typical green tea flavour.

Brewing Tips
Brew 2.5g in 200ml (7fl oz) water at 87°C (190°F) for 3–4 minutes. Strain and add more water for a second and third infusion.

One of Taiwan's finest oolongs, Tung Ting is made with young leaves gathered on the highest plantations above Sungpoling (Pine Bluff). The bushes grow on a hilly plateau that is sheltered by groves of areca palm and giant bamboo.

Character
The young leaves and buds brew a pale greeny-golden cup that has a superb flavour and a subtle floral aroma. It is one of the finest green oolongs.

Brewing Tips
Brew 3g in 200ml (7fl oz) water at 85°C (185°F) for 1–2 minutes. Strain and add more water for several more short steepings.

Taiwan

Yu Oolong (Jade Oolong)

This is a lightly fermented oolong from Yi Lan county.

Character
The rich, green, loosely rolled leaves yield a tawny infusion that has a complex, delicate, floral aroma and flavour and a deliciously smooth finish.

Brewing Tips
Brew 3g in 200ml (7fl oz) water at 85°C (185°F) for 1–2 minutes. Strain and add more water for several further short infusions.

Bao Zhong (Jade Pouchong)

Not truly a green, yet not wholly an oolong, pouchongs are oxidized in a unique way. They are wrapped in cloth or paper to keep the leaves moist for longer during the heat-generated oxidation. Most pouchongs are oxidized 12%–18%.

Character
The tea yields a delicate, sweet aroma and a slightly sweet, delicate, smooth flavour. This is a very relaxing and satisfying cup.

Brewing Tips
For the best results, brew 2.5–3g in 200ml (7fl oz) water at 85°C (185°F) to give multiple short infusions.

Dong Fang Mei Ren (Oriental Beauty, White Monkey Oolong)

This was originally devised to compete with the popular teas from Darjeeling. It was promoted heavily in Europe and the United States before World War II. The tea is only picked once a year, at the end of summer.

Character
This is a fragrant tea with all the complexities of an oolong in both taste and aroma but with the appearance and strength of a black tea.

Brewing Tips
Brew 2.5–3g in 200ml (7fl oz) water at 85°C (185°F) to give multiple short infusions.

Tarry Lapsang Souchong

Taiwan Lapsang Souchongs tend to have a more tarry and pungent aroma and flavour than Chinese Lapsangs.

Character
The large-leafed, slate-black, smoked tea yields a richly smoky aroma and a distinctive full-bodied flavour that is long in the mouth.

Brewing Tips
Infuse 2.5g in 200ml (7fl oz) water at 100°C (212°F) for 3–4 minutes.

Taiwan

Argentina

Argentina has been producing tea since the 1950s, mainly in the Misiones region in the north-east of the country. Because of a shortage of labour, all the harvesting is carried out by large tractor-like machines which trundle between the rows of tea bushes. The teas give a dark liquor that has a plain, somewhat earthy taste and medium body.

Australia

First attempts at tea-growing were in the late 1800s but plants were washed away by a cyclone and tidal wave and no further attempts were made to grow tea commercially until 1959. In 1978, a new company, Madura Tea Estates, was established to grow tea in New South Wales. A mixture of both the Assam and Chinese variety of the tea plant is culti- vated and the organically grown teas are generally blended with quality organic Ceylons and Assams to create a range of black, green and flavoured teas. The Nerada Tea Company markets tea grown on small- holder farms in the Nerada Valley of northern Queensland.

Azerbaijan

Despite suitable growing conditions in the Lenkoran-Astara and Zagatala regions of the country, tea production in Azerbaijan is decreasing. Domestic consumption is high and most of the tea drunk is imported.

Azores

Tea was first brought to the Azores from Brazil in the 1820s but the quality of the tea was never particularly good. In 1984, the government brought in an expert from Mozambique to the island of San Miguel in order to oversee the establishment of new plantations, the introduction of new plants, and new cultivation and manufacturing processes. The industry is very small and most of the tea is sold locally to residents and tourists.

Bangladesh

Tea production in Bangladesh dates back to 1857 when the first garden was planted out at Malnicherra in Sylhet. Today there are 158 gardens and 114 factories, with tea playing an important part in the national economy. The country produces 56,000 tonnes of made tea every year and it is hoped that, with the more widespread use of clonal plants, the modernization of factories and improved infrastructure, production will rise to 90,000 tonnes in the next 15 years. Bangladeshi teas are all black, give good colour and have a strong, sometimes slightly spicy character.

Brazil

Tea-growing was introduced to Brazil in the 1920s by a Japanese immigrant and the tea estates are located in the area to the south-west of São Paulo. Mechanical harvesting produces 10,000 tonnes of black tea that is used in blending.

Burundi

Commercial cultivation of tea started in Burundi in the early 1970s. Initially, production increased at a steady pace but, as in other African states, a history of political instability has negatively affected the industry.

Cameroon

The Germans took the first tea plants to Cameroon in 1914 and planted them at Tole on the fertile slopes of Mount Cameroon. Tole is situated at a height of 600 metres (2,000 feet) above sea level. Conditions here are ideal but recent unrest at the estate means that what were once excellent quality, orthodox black teas are now less readily available.

Democratic Republic of Congo

Black tea is produced in the north-eastern highland region, with an annual production of around just 3,000 tonnes. Although the government has made attempts to increase production, annual output remains low and has in fact dropped since 1978.

Ecuador

Annually, 1,000 tonnes of tea a year are made on the Te Sangay Tea Estate on the 'wrong' side of a 200-metre- (650-foot-) wide river, 915 metres (3,000 feet) up in a stretch of land between the Andes and the Amazon jungle. After manufacture, the tea has to be transported across the river on trolleys that run along a cable to the road, where lorries load it and take it down to the port of Guayaquil.

Ethiopia

Ethiopia is relatively new to tea-growing. First experiments were carried out in the 1930s and since 1978, 2,200 hectares (5,435 acres) have been planted on two state-owned plantations at Wush Wush and Gumero, with further plantings and new factories planned. Until 1989, teas from elsewhere in Africa and China were imported to meet the domestic need but the government established national plantations to help reduce imports. The teas are now beginning to find customers in the European marketplace.

Indonesia

Tea cultivation was started by the Dutch East India Company on Sumatra in the early eighteenth century. The first plants were grown from seed imported from China but they did not flourish and were replaced with Assam bushes brought from India. In the early part of the twentieth century, Indonesian teas dominated the European and British markets. However, the war brought with it a major decline in the industry, which did not recover until the 1980s when a rehabilitation programme began. Since then, there has been constant improvement, modernization of factories and the replanting of old estates, and the Research Institute for Tea has worked with the industry to increase tea production and improve quality. The majority of the tea is grown on plantations located in the highlands of the island of Java on volcanic soil, where the tropical climate encourages vigorous growth. Leaves are plucked throughout the year, with the best quality resulting from the late summer harvest in August and September. In the past all teas were black orthodox but some estates now manufacture CTC teas to meet the growing demand for teabag blends. Green tea production was introduced in the 1980s and now accounts for circa 60% of total output.

Iran

Since the early 1900s, Iran has been producing tea in the northern provinces of Gilan and Mazandaran. There are 57,000 local households now growing tea and selling their green leaf to 134 processing plants that manufacture black teas. The teas give a reddish, light, smooth liquor.

Italy

For hundreds of years, the Cattolica family of Sant-Andrea di Compito has been growing Camellias and in the 1980s, botanist Guido Cattolica started working with the Lucca (Tuscany) Botanical Garden to produce tea in a new experimental tea garden on the family property. Green teas are produced by the Japanese method of steaming, drying and rolling and Cattolica is now experimenting with oolongs.

Madagascar
The island's clonal teas are grown at a height of 1,675 metres (5,500 feet) on the Sahambavy tea plantation. The manufactured black teas give a bright coloury tea similar to the best East African teas. Production is seasonal, with growth slowing during the dry season of May to September.

Malaysia
The first tea plantation was established in the Cameron Highlands in 1929 by the son of a British civil servant who named it Boh after Bohea, the mountainous district of China where black tea was made and exported to Europe. Boh produces roughly 70% of Malaysia's tea in what are almost perfect conditions for the tea plant. The orthodox teas produced here give a light, bright smooth liquor and a rich golden colour.

Mauritius
Tea was first introduced to the island of Mauritius in the late 1760s by Frenchman Pierre Poivre. Since commercial production started in the 1960s, the Mauritius Tea Factories Company has been established to manage four factories owned by the Tea Development Authority. Economic pressures, high costs and high world tea prices have created problems for the industry and the government is currently considering other uses for land currently under tea.

Mozambique
Tea is grown in the agricultural Zambezi region of the country but production has declined over the past 30 years due to political unrest. The strong black teas are generally used in blends for teabags.

Papua New Guinea
Conditions of both climate and soil in Papua New Guinea are ideal for tea and the plant has been grown in the Western Highlands here since the 1800s. The mostly black teas are sold abroad for use in blends.

Russia

Cultivation goes back to 1833 when tea seeds were planted at Nikity Botanical Garden in the Crimea. After the Second World War, the industry expanded rapidly. The growing area is in Krasnodar province in the south-west of the country but production is low and quality poor.

Rwanda

The Rwandan tea industry was established in the 1950s and, with fertile soil and plentiful rainfall, tea flourished here. However, the civil war of the 1990s led to the complete demise of the industry and although some good tea has been produced since 1995, quality is not consistent.

South Africa

The first tea plants, brought from Kew Gardens in London, were planted in 1850 in Durban Botanical Gardens, Natal. Commercial cultivation started in 1877 using seeds from Assam and since then estates have been planted out in Kwa-Zulu-Natal (1959), in the Drakensberg Mountains in Eastern Transvaal, in other parts of Natal, in Transkei (1960s), in the Levubu area, in Venda and in central Zululand near Ntingwe (since 1973). Leaf is harvested during the short rainy season from November to March and most is processed into black tea by a modified CTC method. South Africa is also now famous for the production of Rooibos (also known as Rositea or Red Tea), which is processed from the leaf of the *Aspalathus linoaris*, not from the *Camellia sinensis*.

South Korea

South Korea has plantations in various locations south of Chonju. The most important estates are in Posong near Kangjin and on the slopes of Wolch'ul-san in the south-west. The rows of bushes look rather like those grown in Japan in that the plucking table is smoothly rounded rather than flat. The leaves and buds are gathered in April and May, with the earliest harvest producing the finest flavour. All the teas are green and manufacturing methods vary. For Puch'o-ch'a the leaves are softened in an iron pan over a wood fire, rubbed and rolled to make them curl, then fired again. This is repeated up to nine times until the leaves are dry. For Chung-ch'a the leaves are plunged into almost boiling water, drained and then placed in a large pan over an open fire and rolled and rubbed by hand (the workers wear gloves) until dry.

Tanzania

German settlers were the first to grow tea at Amari and Rungwa in the early 1900s. Commercial production started in 1926 and the industry expanded steadily in the Southern Highlands and the Usambaras. The industry operates on two levels – private estates that grow and manufacture their own tea and smallholder farmers who sell their leaf to state-owned factories run by the Tanzania Tea Authority. Production varies from year to year depending on labour shortages, transportation problems, weather patterns, etc., and quality varies according to altitude and plucking standards. The black teas produced are all good-quality CTC and fetch average prices on world markets.

Tibet

Tibet has grown tea since the days of China's Tang Dynasty (AD618–906) and today the All-The-Tea Company produces organic green tea at the Yigong Tea Plantation in Linzhi Prefecture. The plantation lies at an altitude of 3,650 metres (12,000 feet) amongst high mountain peaks where the cool misty conditions are excellent for the tea bushes. Because of the high elevation, the tea is only harvested during one season each year.

Turkey

Since 1938, Turkey has been growing tea in the Rize district close to the Black Sea. The 60,000 farming families and local factories produce medium-grade tea that gives a dark liquor and a gentle, almost sweet flavour. Turkish tea is mostly consumed domestically.

Uganda

Tea was introduced into the Botanic Gardens at Entebbe, Uganda, in 1909 but there was no commercial cultivation until the late 1920s when Brooke Bond began extensive planting. From the mid-1950s there was rapid expansion, and by the early 1970s tea had become the country's most important export. Political instability in the 1970s and '80s brought a major decline but since 1989 a major rehabilitation of the plantations and factories has brought increased output. Ugandan teas are all black and most are exported for use in teabag blends.

United Kingdom

A small tea plantation is being carefully nurtured in the warm balmy climate of Cornwall in the extreme south-west of Britain. Camellias have grown here in the open for more than a hundred years and the first experimental seedlings of the *Camellia sinensis* were planted at Tregothnan three years ago by the Boscawen family. Money from the European Union is helping to pay for the trials and to train staff.

United States

The Americans first tried to grow tea in the nineteenth century on Wadmalaw Island off the coast of South Carolina. After a brief ownership, in 1987 Lipton sold its Charleston Tea Plantation to a private company that produced 'American Classic Tea'. In 2003, the American tea company, Bigelow, purchased the estate and has renamed it Charleston Tea Gardens.

Vietnam

Vietnam has been growing tea since 1825 when the French established plantations. With continuous political unrest in the region, the industry suffered badly and it was not until the 1990s that foreign investment and rehabilitation brought an increase in production and quality. Today, approximately 80,000 tonnes of both black and green tea are manufactured every year and several flavoured varieties, including jasmine, lotus and chrysanthemum, are now also offered. The bulk of green teas are consumed domestically and black varieties are mostly exported. The country has plans to triple tea exports by 2010.

Zimbabwe

Tea cultivation started here in the 1960s and there are now two main tea-growing areas – in Chipinge and Honde Valley in the south-east of the country. Rainfall is low, at only about 66 centimetres (26 inches) a year, whereas 127 centimetres (50 inches) is required. An efficient irrigation system is essential and the cold winter season means that the bush only grows from spring through to autumn. All the tea produced is black and is mostly exported for blending.

The Chinese drink green tea as their national everyday beverage, just as they did centuries ago, and offer a bowlful to all guests upon arrival in the home. In some houses, the traditional 'gongfu' ceremony is performed using a set of delicate tea bowls, straight-sided smelling cups, a small earthenware teapot and the traditional method of making several infusions from the same measure of leaves, each with its own individual aroma and flavour. Chinese social life still centres around the tea house, where people of all types and ages mingle, drink tea, and catch up with the latest gossip. The different teas are brewed in glasses, guywans or teapots, with additional water often poured onto the same leaves to give several infusions. A waiter moves around the room, dispensing more water from a kettle with a long spout.

In Tibet tea is churned with goat's milk and yak butter.

In Mongolia, 'brick' tea (see page 40) is crushed and brewed with water and yak butter-milk, the liquor is then strained and mixed with milk, salt, butter and roasted grain. In Tibet, brick tea is crushed and soaked in water overnight and the infusion is then churned with salt, goat's milk and yak butter to produce a thick buttery drink. Sometimes a handful or two of grain is added to make a nourishing, soup-like food known as 'tsampa'. Both Mongolian and Tibetan tea are drunk from a bowl rather than a cup.

The Russians have always traditionally brewed their tea with a samovar – an urn that developed from the Mongolian cooking stove and that consists of a pot set on top of a tall chimney sitting over a fire (as in Japan and Europe, the local tea-drinkers adapted the method of brewing that they learnt from the Chinese to suit their own cooking methods and equipment). A little pot of black tea is brewed very strong and then placed, to keep warm, on the top of the samovar. When tea is served, a cup is half filled with the

A Russian couple drink from a samovar

strong tea, watered down with hot water drawn from the tap in the side of the samovar, and drunk with sugar or jam.

In Turkey, a strong black brew is prepared and strained into tulip-shaped glasses and served with little sweetmeats. In the eastern part of the country, a cube of sugar is placed under the tongue before the tea is sipped from the glass. Some Turks drink so much tea that they carry a 'semover', like a Russian samovar, in the back of their car so to always be able to boil water for tea. In domestic life, tea has great importance; mothers always ensure their daughters know how to brew tea correctly.

In Iran and Afghanistan, tea is the national beverage. Both green and black are used – green as a refreshing thirst quencher and black as a warming, comforting brew, and both types are taken with sugar. At home and in the popular tea houses, drinkers sit cross-legged on floormats and sip their tea from glasses or elegant porcelain bowls.

Moroccans have also drunk tea for centuries, having learnt the custom from early Arab traders, and consider it an important part of any social or business occasion. At a Moroccan tea-drinking ceremony incense is lit, and all those taking part wash their hands in orange blossom water and watch while the host prepares the tea. Green tea, fresh mint and sugar are measured into a tall silver pot and hot water is then poured in. Little glasses are set ready on a tray and when the tea has brewed, the golden liquor is poured from a height so that it froths into the glasses and settles with a layer of tiny bubbles on the surface. Accompanying nibbles include dried apricots, figs and nuts.

In Egypt, the Bedouin version of the drink is made by boiling tea leaves and sweetening the infusion with plenty of sugar. Tea is also flavoured with dried mint leaves and served with sugar in glasses.

In Japan, the traditional Green Tea Ceremony (see page 74) is still an important social ritual and the ability to perform it is considered an essential skill for well-educated young ladies. Although the most popular tea is still green, many Japanese today also enjoy black tea drunk in the British way with milk. Since the 1980s, many British-style tea-rooms have opened in which traditional afternoon tea is served with sandwiches, scones and clotted cream, and little cakes and pastries. In some metropolitan areas, there are also some very stylish green tea 'cafés' that serve unusual flavoured and blended green teas.

In India, black tea is drunk with milk and sugar. Young boys ('chai wallahs') brew tea on street corners using kettles and brass pots and mix it with buffalo milk and sugar. They sell it to passers-by who drink it from little earthenware cups that are thrown away after use. Spiced tea, known as 'chai' or 'marsala chai' and made with pepper, cinnamon, cardamom, cloves and sugar, is also very popular. 'Afternoon tea', with savoury and sweet snacks, is served in the tea-rooms of India's smart hotels throughout the afternoon.

In Sri Lanka, lunchtime tea with 'hoppers' is a traditional institution. Hoppers are a type of pancake made with rice flour, coconut milk, sugar, salt and yeast and cooked in a special pan to give a bowl shape. They are served with a variety of curries and spicy sauces. In hotels, as in India, 'afternoon tea' is offered through the afternoon.

In Malaysia, tea is brewed very strong and then mixed with thick condensed milk and plenty of sugar. Sometimes the tea and condensed milk are mixed together and then poured several times between two jugs so that the liquid becomes deliciously frothy. The Malaysians also like iced tea, made by pouring strong hot tea and condensed milk over crushed ice.

Selling tea from a street kiosk in Sri Lanka

In the UK, black tea is still the preferred brew for most people but consumption of green and flavoured teas is on the increase. Many people start the day with a cup of tea in bed, more tea at breakfast and lunch and, increasingly, tea after the main meal in the evening. Afternoon tea at 4 or 5pm is still a very important institution, with many families serving it at home at the weekend, and all the major hotels around the country offering pots of tea served with neat little sandwiches, scones with jam and cream and a selection of elegant pastries and cakes.

In the United Kingdom

Amber McCarroll
c/o the Tea Council (see opposite)
Tel: (00 44) (0) 1379 384596
Mobile: (00 44) 07815 774414
email: ambermccarroll@hotmail.com

Tasseologist and writer

Betty's Cafe Tea Rooms
1 Parliament Street
Harrogate
North Yorkshire HG1 2QU
Tel: (00 44) (0) 1423 502746

Traditional tea-rooms and tea retailers with branches in various locations in Yorkshire

Bird on the Rock Tea Room
Abcott
Clungunford
Shropshire SY7 0PX
Tel: (00 44) (0) 1588 660631

Exceptional tea-room and tea retailer; winner of the UK Tea Council's Top Tea Place award 2004

Infuse Tea Ltd
36 Byron Hill Road
Harrow-on-the-Hill
Middlesex HA2 0HY
Tel: (00 44) (0) 20 8426 8064/5

Tea classes for Japanese people in London

... and ...

Shop (shared with St James's Teas Ltd)
202 Blackfriars Road
London SE1 8NJ
email: asteward@infuse-tea.co.uk
www.infuse-tea.co.uk

St James's Teas Ltd
Head Office and Shop
202 Blackfriars Road
London SE1 8NJ
Tel: (00 44) (0) 20 7401 0630/1
Fax: (00 44) (0) 20 7633 0422
email info@stjamesteas.co.uk
www.stjamesteas.co.uk

Retailers and wholesalers of teas from around the world; also offer books on tea and tea accessories

Teacraft
1 Grisedale Court
Woburn Road Industrial Estate
Kempston, Bedford
MK42 7WJ
Tel: (00 44) (0) 1234 852121
Fax: (00 44) (0) 1234 853232
www.teacraft.com

Consultants and technical advisers to the world tea industry

The UK Tea Council
9 The Courtyard
Gowan Avenue
London SW6 6RH
Tel: (00 44) (0) 20 7371 7787
email: tea@teacouncil.co.uk
www.teacouncil.co.uk

Independent body representing major tea-producing countries and UK packers; dedicated to promoting tea

Wilson Smithett
202 Blackfriars Road
London SE1 8NJ
Tel: (00 44) (0) 20 7401 0620
email: info@wilsonsmithett.co.uk
www.wilsonsmithett.co.uk

Tea brokers since 1865 and parent company to St James's Teas Ltd. The company runs regular tea-tasting sessions. For appointments, call 00 44 020 7401 0623

In the United States

Elmwood Inn Fine Teas
205 East 4th Street
Perryville, KY 40468
(00 1) 800-765-2139

*Tea retailers and wholesalers, consultants,
trainers, publishers and book distributors*

Harney & Sons Fine Teas
PO Box 665
Salisbury, CT 06068
(00 1) 888-427-6398
www.harney.com

*Retailers and wholesalers of teas from
around the world; tea-related gifts and
books*

Imperial Tea Court
1411 Powell Street
San Francisco, CA 94133
(00 1) 800-567-5898
www.imperialtea.com

*Specialists in China teas and Chinese tea
accessories*

Peet's Coffee & Tea
PO Box 12509
Berkeley, CA 94712-3509
(00 1) 800-999-2132
www.peets.com

*Tea retailers with locations throughout
North America*

Simpson & Vail, Inc
PO Box 765
3 Quarry Rd
Brookfield, CT 06804
(00 1) 203-775-0240
www.svtea.com

*Tea wholesalers and retailers offering a
wide range of tea, tea-related gifts, books,
linens*

The Tea House
541 Fessler Avenue
Naperville, IL 60565
(00 1) 630-961-0877
www.theteahouse.com

*Importers, blenders and retailers of the
world's finest teas and accessories; specialists in Chinese and Taiwanese teas*

Tea Source
752 Cleveland Ave. So.
St Paul, MN 55116
(00 1) 651-690-9822
www.teasource.com

Tea retail counters and tea bars

Teavana
(00 1) 404-995-8203
www.teavana.com

Tea bars and retail counters in locations
throughout North America

Upton Tea Imports
34-A Hayden Rowe Street
Hopkinton, MA 01748
(00 1) 508-435-9922
www.uptontea.com

Tea importers and retailers

Rest of the World

Babingtons
Piazza de Spagna 23
Rome 00187
Italy
Tel: (00 39) 6 67 866 027

English-style tea-room and tea retailer in
the centre of Rome

Georgia Tea
The Producer Farmers Association
Caucasus Tea
Georgia
Kutaisi, 4600
Rustaveli Avenue #179
email: imereti@sanetk.net.ge
www.georgia-tea.com

Hand- and machine-made teas produced by
local families

Marco Polo Products Pte Ltd
79 Chitrakoot Building
230-A AJC Bose Road
Calcutta 700 020
Tel: (00 91) 33 2247 1036
Fax: (00 91) 33 2247 7508
email: goomtee@darjeelingteas.com

Tea planters and wholesalers – owners of
Goomtee and Jungpana estates

Mariage Frères
13 rue des Grands-Augustins
Paris 75006
France
Tel: (00 33) 1 40 51 82 50

Tea-rooms and tea retail counters in three locations in Paris

Ming Cha
Leekwan Tea Trade Ltd
1 Hoi Wan Street
China Chem Exchange Square
#703 Quarry Bay
Hong Kong
Tel: (00 852) 2882 98123
Fax: (00 852) 2577 9117
email: enquiry@mingcha.com.hk
www.mingcha.com.hk

Specialists in Chinese oolongs, puerhs and other Chinese teas

Wijs & Zonen
Warmoesstraat 102
1012 JJ Amsterdam
The Netherlands
Tel: (00 31) 20 624 0436
Fax: (00 31) 20 625 6648
email: info@wijs-zonen.nl

Speciality tea merchants

Inproc
Denneweg 126
2514 CL Den Haag
The Netherlands
Tel: (00 31) 70 346 1541
email: inproc@koffietuin.nl

Speciality tea merchants

Fa.wed.A.Garsen – de Pelikaan
Pelikaanstraat 9
7201 DR Zutphen
The Netherlands
Tel: (00 31) 575 512 024
Fax: (00 31) 575 541 750
email: pelikaan-wed.a.garsen@planet.nl

Speciality tea merchants

Simon Lévelt Koffiebranderij en Theehandel
A. Hofmanweg 3
2031 BH Haarlem
Tel: (00 31) 235 122 522
Fax: (00 31) 235 122 505
www.simonlevelt.com

*28 speciality shops covering most
major Dutch towns*

INDEX

Page numbers in **bold** indicate main entries in the Directory sections.